THE POCKET BOOK OF PROOFREADING

By the same author
HOLD YOUR HEAD UP HIGH

THE POCKET BOOK OF PROOFREADING

:::

A Guide to Freelance Proofreading & Copy-editing

WILLIAM CRITCHLEY

 FIRST ENGLISH BOOKS

First published in Great Britain in 2007 by:
First English Books, 22 Hive Gardens,
Poole BH13 7PD

The right of William Critchley to be identified as the author of this work has been asserted by him in accordance with the Copyright, Designs and Patents Act, 1988.

No part of this publication may be reproduced, stored in a retrieval system, or transmitted in any form or by any means, electronic, mechanical, photocopying, recording, or otherwise without the prior permission of the publisher. All rights reserved.

ISBN-13: 978-0-9551437-2-4

Book production: Melinda Sandell
Cover design: Juliet Martin; Pentacor.co.uk
Digital annotation and website design/programming: Bart Nagel
Copy-editing/proofreading/index: Michèle Clarke
Printed and bound in Great Britain by Antony Rowe Ltd,
East Sussex, in 11pt Sabon/26pt Century Gothic

A CIP catalogue record for this book is available from the British Library.

Copyright © 2007 William Critchley

CONTENTS

For
MARYAM
with love

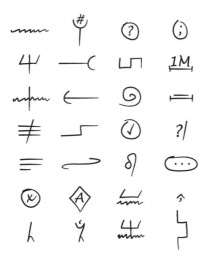

And some of the little helpers

A bliss in proof, —and prov'd, a very woe;
Before, a joy propos'd; behind a dream.

William Shakespeare
Sonnets, 129

Certain things they should stay the way they are.
You ought to be able to stick them in one of those
big glass cases and just leave them alone.

J. D. Salinger
The Catcher in the Rye

Mix a little foolishness with your serious plans:
it's lovely to be silly at the right moment.

Horace, *Odes*, IV

'Lovely William or rather, lovely, William!'

On the importance of a single comma; email from
Michèle Clarke to author (on receipt of draft proofs of
index for *The Pocket Book of Proofreading*), 11 May 2007

Acknowledgements

First English Books gratefully acknowledges permission to reproduce copyright material in this book.

For the picture of the 'impostor' bear on the front cover:
Flower Delivery UK
For the use of 'Marks for copy preparation and proof correction', extracted from BS 5261C:2005, reproduced with permission: British Standards Institution (BSI)
Exercise 1: editorial in *The Times*, 4 August 2006, reproduced with permission, The Times/NI Syndication. © NI Syndication, London (4 August 2006)
Exercise 3: Rena Salman, from *Greek Food* (Fontana, London, 1983)
Exercise 4: Robert Payne, from *The Splendour of Greece* (Pan Books, London, 1964)
'To a Poet a Thousand Years Hence' is from *An Anthology of Modern Verse*. Ed. A. Methuen (Methuen & Co., London, 1921)
Photo of Archibald Ormsby-Gore: reproduced courtesy of The Times/Leon Neal, NI Syndication, and with permission from the Betjeman estate. © NI Syndication, London (28 August 2006)
Photo of Eva Longoria: reproduced courtesy of The Times/Chris Harris and NI Syndication. © NI Syndication, London (29 December 2006)

Every effort has been made to contact copyright owners for permission to quote copyright material, and the publisher apologises for any omissions. Any errors, oversights or omissions will be corrected in subsequent editions.

Preface

I'm surprised no one else has brought out a book called *The Pocket Book of Proofreading*. There are times when it's handy to be able to refer to a reference book for various sorts of queries on the subject of proofreading. Where do you start?

This book will make a good beginning. If you need to ensure that what you write is correct, you'll find something of interest in this slim volume.

I spent a number of enjoyable years working as a freelance proofreader and copy-editor. For most of that time at least six typescripts and/or proofs were piled high on my desk. The money wasn't bad. Like many people, I 'fell' into the work by chance, in my case when a sister brought home a bulky set of proofs (she'd just found a job with a London publisher). She decided she didn't like the work so I volunteered. Of course, I hadn't the vaguest idea about what marks to use to correct the proofs, but my sister gave me a friend's phone number, and he taught me the most common marks in use in about twenty minutes. I was in!

The warning must be that it's not that easy to get started. If only, you might think, some kind publisher would throw a pile of proofs your way once a week, you could earn enough to get by...find two or three publishers, and you could even pay the mortgage.

So, what do you need to get started? A big slice of luck, application, dedication, good reading and editing skills, an eye for detail, and a determination to succeed. You might just do it. You could be lucky, but don't count on it.

I know many people have enjoyed working on the proofs of Santorini – A Greek Island. It's more fun than working on the proofs of an academic textbook – full of figures and tables, and enough notes and bibliographical references to induce a yawning fit for the rest of the afternoon.

The only tale I'd like to tell you, briefly, is how I came by the story. It was a long time ago. I was walking along a beach, a strip of black volcanic sand, hot from the beating summer sun. The place was called Perissa, then a fishing village on the island of Santorini in the Cyclades.

I had innocently met a slip of a girl a few days earlier, eyes sloe-black, skin olive-brown. Most of all I remember her slender figure in a turquoise bikini, and eyes that in the clear Greek sunlight spoke of timeless mysteries, a strange fusion of passion and reason. As she walked out of the sea after playing with the waves,* I asked myself if she were more like an Egyptian than a Greek goddess, especially when I saw her profile, the orbs of her eyes like dark moons.

She was neither, just a girl, a young girl, but it was pleasant to sit next to her, hear her soft laughter, and be made to feel 'equal of the gods' (as Sappho recounts in one of her more famous fragments†).

The girl's uncle was fishing on the same stretch of beach. He hadn't caught anything all day. He rushed up, got a pen from someone, then gave me a book, after inscribing his name inside the front cover, and writing, 'To my friend William'. His book was the best present I ever had. I didn't realise at the time how much it would change my life.

I told him I'd give him a copy of the book I'd write some day.

He died not long after, and the girl got married, and had three children, and I've seen her only once in the last twelve years.

Although I still prefer BS 1219 rather than BS 5261C:1976 (see pp. 105–7), the time when a proofreader could use either for 'copy preparation and proof correction' has gone. From April 2006, you must use BS 5261C:2005. It was somehow more arcanely satisfying to write 'stet' in the margin(s) of proofs. Now there's just a tick in a circle; there's a very slight feeling of dumbing down.

If any errors remain, these are my responsibility. It was a habit of mine to escape from any accountability for mistakes by saying it helped people to become better proofreaders, if they found the errors I missed. That's my story, and I'm sticking to it.

Just a note about the bear on the cover. He's not the real 'Archie', of course, but I still like him (the real one being Archibald Ormsby-Gore, longtime companion of Sir John Betjeman). Above the bear is an eclectic selection – from Archie, to three words from a Shakespearean sonnet, to an actress with a part in *Desperate Housewives*. (Alas, actress Eva Longoria was deleted from the cover (see pp. 134 and 199) but she's still very much alive on other pages in this book.) You'll find that proofreading (and copy-editing) will teach you new ways of looking at words.

William Critchley
Canford Cliffs, June 2007

*How can you play with the waves? As I drifted on my back in the beautiful blue water, the girl swam to my side saying, 'Don't you play with the waves?'
†Fragment 31.

Author's Note

I approached several publishers to enquire about their possible interest in *The Pocket Book of Proofreading*. Arousing interest was rather like attempting to resuscitate a moribund diner, or literary hack of an agent, slumped over a literary lunch at the Café Royal. A wall of silence descended. Emailing one London publisher, back came an out-of-office auto reply with this line: 'If you are a spammer sending me junk mail I hope you rot in hell for all eternity.'

Be careful if you are a writer and email publishers – they'll often just consider you as spamming. ('Only *solicited* emails, please,' they'll shout.)

So, when I decided to publish the book myself, under the imprint First English Books, I sent the publisher a copy of my book, along with a laminated note he could use as a bookmark. Here it is.

A GIFT

The Publisher
& Managing Director
– Books

Either use it yourself for sarcastic amusement as you speculate on the hopelessness of lost causes or place on your desk in the event you actually meet a spammer – and wish to assault sufficiently to commit to the underworld – or, in case you find yourself ferried over, take a last, longing look at Eva – as you realise one day you could be in a state worse than poor Archie.

WILLIAM CRITCHLEY
10 June 2007

Introduction

Proofreading and editing skills can be learnt as easily and readily as any of the other skills that all of us acquire throughout our lives. It's also fun! You won't make as much money as a property developer but you can earn enough from home to make it worth studying.

If you simply like the idea of working from home as a freelance proofreader, *The Pocket Book of Proofreading* can show you how. If you'd like to improve your income and develop your editing skills, all the essential information is right here.

There are also some mind-bending exercises to download from a new website, www.pocketbookofproofreading.co.uk, including copy-edited typescript, proofs, and corrected proofs of *Santorini – A Greek Island*, all you need to gain some real practice and experience. It's a complete, professional course for anyone who wants to learn about freelance proofreading and/or copy-editing. (Notice the distinction between proofreading and copy-editing (use of hyphen). Don't ask me why but it seems to be the current convention to hyphenate the latter.)

Working in publishing is stimulating and rewarding. Freelancing offers the opportunity, when you find the work, to be sent proofs or 'typescripts' of books through the mail, direct from the publishing house to your home address, either by first-class post or courier, or the Internet. You may be sent anything from a simple textbook to a romantic novel (something like *Just Like Heaven*, or even a re-run of *Jane Eyre*) – just about anything possible to imagine. From the 180,000-plus books published each year, there's bound to be a lot of choice in subject matter. (Despite some groans from authors, books are big business. Sales in the UK have now reached about 300 million volumes annually, worth £2.4 billion.*)

Once you've acquired the skills, you can enjoy the freedom of working from home, choosing your own hours, and you'll get paid for reading and correcting material that is likely to be interesting, as well as 'educational'.

You don't need a degree but should have at least some GCSEs, including English. You'll find that as your confidence grows, you can tackle any subject (assuming a degree of literacy to begin with). The copy-editor should have marked up the typescript for typesetting, and if this has been done correctly, your job is to ensure that the copy-editor's instructions have been carried out exactly, and that the 'house style' of the publisher has been followed (more on this later).

Most books are now computer typeset but copy-editors are still needed, and proofreaders too. If anything, demand is greater because standards in English generally have fallen. Publishers, however, are always trying to find new ways to save money, and one certain way to do this is to use freelances less.

Whether or not standards have fallen, the importance of commas was never more famously illustrated than by Lynne Truss and her book, *Eats, Shoots & Leaves*. A panda eating a bamboo shoot is natural behaviour but eating, and then shooting (with a Colt .45?) is altogether different. An

---

* *Figures current in 2006/7.*

example of laziness, or perhaps ignorance, is the insertion of an apostrophe in *it is* – when the word intended is a possessive pronoun and not a verb. (The verb can be shortened to *it's* (from it is – the apostrophe showing the omission of *i*), but the possessive pronoun is always just *its*. Here's a line seen recently in a property magazine: 'The opinions expressed here are not necessarily those of the magazine and it's editorial staff.' They should know better!)

There have been many testimonials from people who have taken *The Pocket Book of Proofreading*'s three-part course (originally known as Freelance MS). This course was priced at £92 but using the Internet has made it possible to produce the same material for just £30, a saving of over £60. (It's actually £29.99 but who's going to quibble over 1p?) Once you've bought *The Pocket Book of Proofreading*, you can simply download the three main parts of the course, including some free *Extra Exercises*, and print these out yourself (more on this later).

Lots of people have found this course fun to take, and useful for a variety of reasons. You can use it to brush up on some punctuation points too. *The Pocket Book of Proofreading* and the three-part course (the challenging Santorini proofs) with *Extra Exercises* are an invaluable resource if you'd like to learn how to become a freelance proofreader, working from home.

It's easier than you might think to grasp (and master) how the proofreading marks work. It's not so easy to find work, however. You have to be determined, just as much as you would if you were hired to take part in the TV series, *The Apprentice* (though this isn't exactly a fair analogy because as a freelance you can pick and choose).

You're not dependent on the whim of an employer like Sir Alan Sugar but on your own skills and ability to attract work from in-house editors.

No matter how keen you are, in the real world competition makes life that bit tougher. When I tried to find an indexer and a proofreader to help with this book, it was more difficult than I imagined. Most of the people who were any good were unable to help for at least two to three weeks because they were too busy with work. Bear in mind, when starting out, that you need to keep practising and developing your skills, and that being second rate is never good enough.

To be a successful proofreader you'll need to be almost as picky with the details as Ben Schott is with his *Miscellanies* and *Almanacs*. A perfectionist, he's quoted as saying he feels responsibility (in his books) for 'every last comma'. How else can you learn to deal with accepting or rejecting such quantities of minutiae?

Your first set of proofs is the goal. Be prepared for disappointment and upsets along the way but remember that, ultimately, perseverance pays off.

May good luck fall upon you.

Note: all was well with the guy who wanted me to rot in hell – if I were a spammer. He actually wrote back a while later: 'I am grateful for the gift [the bookmark]. . . You seem to be doing an admirable job with the book anyway. With best wishes for the book, and thank you again.'

CHAPTER 1

What skills are required?

First of all, you don't need to be brilliant with words but a flair for their correct use is important. You'll be expected to have a good 'command' of the English language, be able to spell correctly, and have an eye for detail. (Can you see, for example, what is 'wrong' with the punctuation in this sentence?). If you haven't seen it, the only thing 'wrong' with it is that there's no need for a full point – a full stop (US: period) – at the very end. The punctuation is complete within the parentheses (the round brackets). It's a grammatically correct sentence beginning with a capital letter. Thus the extra full point (there is one in the 'body' of the question mark) amounts to double punctuation. In this sentence, the full point is placed outside the parentheses (for example).

This is just one instance of a rule that can be learnt along with a host of others, all of them basic to editing skills, but they are rules that you can learn quickly and easily, and with practice scarcely even notice as you correct them.

Human error plays its part in the process. The author who wrote/typed the manuscript (i.e. typescript) is not always infallible; the copy-editor who edits the typescript will probably miss a few, if less obvious, errors; the typesetter inputting the text via computer, which will make up the page proofs, will undoubtedly, sometimes disastrously, press the wrong keys, forget certain items, misread one figure for another, mistakenly insert additional keystrokes, make the page 'depth' too short or too long, and generally leave a number of errors (even with computer typesetting), which the proofreader must find and correct, with something like vigilance and skill. (Note that in some respects this is an old-fashioned way of considering book production because, apart from offerings from a few die-hard eccentrics, nearly all MSS today are typescripts, and the copy-editor will do the copy-editing on screen. As the typesetter does not actually 're-type', no further errors should be introduced at this stage.) When the page proofs have been corrected for the final time, the pages will be bound and the book published.

Apart from this human error, computers used in publishing do suffer sporadic glitches, and a sharp-eyed proofreader will be needed to pick up these errors. Spellcheckers are a great help but they have their limitations.

If you're going to work as a freelance, you'll need a certain amount of self-discipline. (Generally, the word is 'freelance' in the UK but 'freelancer' in the US. Either can be used.) You have to decide to work the hours that suit you best. Also, most publishing houses have to work to tight schedules. If a subject or author is popular, or publication is timed to coincide with an important event (such as the Christmas 'list' or the start of the school term), deadlines have to be met. You may be asked to return the proofs by a certain date, sometimes far sooner than the usual time allowed, which is about three to four weeks. However, you will typically be asked if you have the time to spare, and it usually pays to say 'yes', even if you are busy with another set of proofs. Set aside a few more hours to finish the proofs you are currently working on, so you'll have time to complete the next ones, and you can look forward to another cheque towards the end of the following month.

You should also keep in mind the fact that working freelance also involves responsibility. Once you have agreed to work on a particular set of proofs, your in-house editor will be relying on you to see that the proofs are corrected properly, and that they'll be returned by the agreed date. If you're short of time, it's always possible to phone, fax or email and ask for an extra day or two to complete the work. This is as a rule accepted without question – unless there has been a specific agreement that the proofs will be ready 'by 10.00 a.m. on Monday morning'. It does mean, naturally, that you won't be able to rush away on holiday for a couple of weeks until you have completed the work in hand.

CHAPTER 2

Stages in the production process

When the author has submitted a manuscript/typescript and it has been accepted for publication, the in-house or freelance copy-editor will begin work. He or she will have to ensure that:

- a consistent house style is followed throughout
- the various headings and subheadings are given their correct 'weight'
- literals (misspellings in the text) are corrected
- the manuscript is 'marked up' to ensure that the typesetter follows the correct procedure regarding layout, design treatment, style for quotations, font size, etc.
- the typescript reads 'for sense' throughout (that is, the author expresses what he or she is 'saying' as clearly as possible).

A checklist of tasks for both copy-editors and proofreaders is given later in Chapters 16 and 18.

When the typescript has been copy-edited the typesetter will 'set' the text or copy to produce page proofs. Most books go straight into page proofs but a few may also have a galley-proof stage, at which time any essential corrections are made. (A galley proof – rare nowadays – is a proof taken before the text is made up into pages.) Computer typesetting and digital 'print on demand' (POD) have simplified the process considerably.

The page proofs are usually the ones you will receive as a freelance proofreader. The author also gets a copy to check through, and any corrections are then collated later with the proofreader's copy. This means that corrections from the author's copy are transferred to the proofreader's set (if she/he has missed anything) and this is then known as the master set. The proofs are returned to the typesetter and the final corrections are made. There is still work to be done by printers, jacket designers, jacket laminators, binders and so on, but none of this will concern the proofreader or copy-editor.

The proofreader traditionally 'marks up' the various typesetting errors in red but if he/she notices errors that slipped past the copy-editor, these will be marked in blue or black – a good biro or fine, felt-tipped pen (0.5mm) is best. Additional corrections that the author wants to make are usually marked in black; the reason for the different colours is that the typesetter cannot charge for his own mistakes, but corrections added later, or subsequent alterations or additions made by the author will be charged for by the typesetter or printer.

Authors may also be charged for proof corrections that cost more than 10 per cent of the original cost of composition, or at a set rate per hour or part hour. Once again, computer typesetting and digital print on demand have made life *so* much easier. Some copy-editors will edit on-screen. Digital printers can now 'set' pages with Adobe's PDF (Portable Document Format), and simply print from this. Copy-editors need experience and training in order to edit on-screen. They must input any text corrections, and then return the corrected disk(s) to the publisher.

The Internet has also provided many new opportunities. Authors or in-house editors can email several chapters or a complete book to a copy-editor – either living or working 'next door' or on the other side of the world – in virtually no time at all and for minimal cost.

CHAPTER 3

What are the 'tools of the trade'?

For proofreading or copy-editing in general you will need:

- A pencil.
- Red and blue pens. Fine, felt-tipped 0.5mm pens are ideal. Look for a good stationer or your local newsagent. Try to find a pen that doesn't run too easily, one that you feel comfortable with, and fairly finely pointed so that you can achieve a high degree of legibility, and be able to insert a mark, for example, between letters.
- A rubber. As you read the proofs, mark any words you're unsure of, or better still make a fine line in the margin (in pencil), just enough to notice. As you progress through the proofs, you may find the problem resolves itself, and then you can refer back quickly, make the correction, and erase the pencil mark. The copy-editor, for example, may have decided to spell 'judgement' with an 'e' from page or folio 60 onwards, but on pages 22 and 30 might not have noticed 'judgment'. You may find a name

like 'Whiteley', also occurring elsewhere as 'Whitely'. Until you check, you can't be sure which is correct but if you make a small mark in the margin (and keep a note of the page number), you'll be able to find the word again soon enough. Also mark in the margin with a pencilled question mark items you cannot resolve, and which need to be referred to the author. For example, the author may have spelt in the Bibliography another author's name as 'Granger' but it may appear in the text as 'Grainger'. You won't have the time to check which is correct but you can send in a list of queries to your in-house editor when returning the proofs.

- To provide anything like a professional service, you'll need a standard PC with printer. Familiarity with Microsoft Word helps. You'll need them to:
  - send back a list of queries (if any)
  - send a covering letter to the editor who sent you the proofs
  - send in an invoice for hours worked.
- Reference books (see Chapter 4).
- A good-sized desk where you can work comfortably without getting too tired, or too cramped, and a good reading light. The latter will help your eyes and help you to 'focus' and direct your attention to the proofs (or so you hope!).

To recap: pencil, red and blue pens, your PC with printer, reference books, and phone or fax and/or email. Add to this short list a clear head in the morning. Some people like a ruler to place under each printed line for ease of reading.

Reading proofs (copy-editing too) requires prolonged attention to detail and good concentration. Take a break and chill. Make some tea or coffee or surf the Net for your favourite URLs! Put your iPod on shuffle and relax or dream about what you could do with Apple's new iPhone – said to be 'five years ahead of any other mobile phone'. Publishers don't expect their readers to scan 50,000 words and consistently achieve 100 per cent accuracy, but they will naturally be upset (and sometimes ruthless) if you have not made a real effort. The best way to achieve this is to adopt a professional approach from the beginning.

CHAPTER 4

Reference books

The main requirement is a standard dictionary such as the *Shorter* (or *Concise*) *Oxford Dictionary*. In cases of doubtful spelling, you'll need a dictionary to hand to which you can refer with the minimum of effort. It often helps to have a second dictionary as a back up, or to compare spellings. Choose one that is large enough to cope with your needs. Try *Collins English Dictionary* or the *Concise Oxford English Dictionary*.

An essential book, which is also inexpensive, is the *New Oxford Dictionary for Writers and Editors: The Essential A–Z Guide to the Written Word*. This replaces *The Oxford Writers' Dictionary*, previously published as *The Oxford Dictionary for Writers and Editors*. You can also use this for spelling, especially when there are alternative ways of spelling a word. It gives guidance on a host of subjects that you'll meet in your work; for example, foreign words not in common use should be in italics, and the *New Oxford Dictionary for Writers and Editors* gives guidance on this, which can be followed. *New Hart's Rules: The Handbook of Style for Writers and Editors*, previously known as *Hart's Rules for Compositors and Readers*, published by Oxford University Press, has a useful list of hyphenated and non-hyphenated words, as has the *Oxford Minidictionary of Spelling*, which gives sensible word breaks for ends of lines. However, the *New Oxford Dictionary for Writers and Editors* is probably just as good.

For an extensive list of proofreader's marks, see the British Standards Institution (BSI), *Copy Preparation and Proof Correction*, BS 5261C:2005. However, once you have become aware of the more familiar marks, and have learnt how they are used, it is unwise to become too complicated in your approach.

You have to ensure that the typesetter or digital printer can understand your instructions, so consistency and clarity of style are just as important as having an extensive knowledge of every possible mark.

The *Writers' & Artists' Yearbook*, published annually, has a useful list of proofreader's marks with explanations. This paperback is an essential book, which you will need later: it contains hundreds of business addresses, names, and email contacts for a huge number of publishers in the UK and abroad.

Editors (and proofreaders) will find a thesaurus useful (several publishers sell them), particularly when an author has the annoying habit of using the same set of adjectives *ad infinitum*. Some authors, for example, may describe every step taken as 'positive' or 'concrete' or keep repeating a phrase or sentence, such as, 'I'll have some of that', or 'Computer says no', and the copy-editor might need to provide alternatives. (Try the thesaurus on your PC. Highlight the word or phrase in Word, right click for Synonyms.)

Judith Butcher's *Copy-editing: The Cambridge Handbook for Editors, Authors and Publishers* is an indispensable book (published by Cambridge University Press) but it is expensive. ('From the basics of how to mark a typescript for the designer and typesetter, through the ground rules of house style and consistency, to how to read and correct proofs, *Copy-Editing* covers all aspects of the editorial processes involved in converting author's typescript to printed page.')

Notice how in the last quote, the part-title, *Copy-Editing*, does not agree with the previous title, *Copy-editing*. Train yourself to be aware of possible inconsistencies. Anyway, a new edition has been published. Some proofreaders (and copy-editors) insist on buying only the most up-to-date editions. Several of the books listed in this chapter might have been superseded by the time you read this. Apologies if this is the case – the world is changing so fast – like nanoseconds are *so* last year! I don't see what's wrong with slightly less recent editions, and they are probably cheaper.

It's true that any reference book you use constantly is going to get bruised and battered around the edges, and the contents age with time's passing, like Sir John Betjeman's ancient old teddy bear, Archibald Ormsby-Gore (better known as Archie). The unfortunate problem is that most reference books need updating regularly but, just as no one could, or should have, 'updated' Archibald, I still look affectionately upon certain older reference books of mine. They're frayed and tattered, their spines no longer crisp and upright but does that matter? Inside there is pure gold dust.

It can take years sometimes for changes to occur in the use of words. A quick glance at a cookery book published forty years ago swiftly unearths six uses of hyphens that have gone: grape-fruit, bay-leaf, curry-powder, horse-radish, shell-fish, left-overs. In the country, you'd pick blackberries but gorge on red- and black-currants! Is this an excuse to hang on to old books that still have life left in them? You'll need to replace them with newer models soon. ('Oh, Archie,' I can hear John Betjeman saying, 'does it have to end like this?')

Another good book is the *New Oxford Spelling Dictionary: The Writers' and Editors' Guide to Spelling and Word Division*. There's also the *Oxford A–Z of Grammar and Punctuation* by John Seely, less than a fiver from Amazon, 168 pages, published by Oxford University Press.

A classy book is the *Oxford Style Manual*, which has a hefty price tag but you can buy it for much less on Amazon. ('*The Oxford Style Manual* combines in one volume the two essential reference works that every writer should possess, *The Oxford Dictionary for Writers and Editors* and the *Oxford Guide to Style*.') The book is 'an essential reference tool for authors and publishers, copy-editors, proofreaders, copywriters, and those who write websites – indeed anyone who cares about using the English language well'. However, mistakes abounded in an OUP earlier *Style Manual*, so the main recommendation has to be the *Writers' Reference Pack* (see below for details of the new set).

With so many scribes scribbling away, and Lynne Truss's zero tolerance of bad punctuation, you can bet that as soon as a new reference book comes out, talented and dedicated proofreaders will start 'ganging up' to find the errors. The OUP and CUP must get a lot of their work done free. There are some proofreaders out there who just can't sleep because they're tut-tutting over tiny mistakes in the latest reference books.

(In the United States, editors, copy-editors and proofreaders use different reference books. One of the most famous is *The Chicago Manual of Style*.)

Perhaps the best buy is the *Writers' Reference Pack* consisting of *New Hart's Rules*, *New Oxford Dictionary for Writers and Editors*, and the *New Oxford Spelling Dictionary*, that's three books in one for a total of £30!

Occasionally you may have to proofread extracts of poetry and here it is always a good idea to have one or two poetry anthologies to check the correctness of entries.

Another good book is *Basic Editing: A Practical Course* by Nicola Harris. It's not a book for proofreaders but you'll certainly pick up some useful tips and ideas. You can also learn a lot from *Freelance Proofreading and Copy-editing* by Trevor Horwood. This A4-size book costs £15 from Action Print Press.

To sum up: don't rush out and buy every book you can find. You can manage pretty well with a good dictionary, and the *New Oxford Dictionary for Writers and Editors*. (**Note:** if your grammar is shaky, get hold of a copy of the new *Compact Oxford English Dictionary for Students*. Students may get better grades but the basics of good grammar elude them. This dictionary was compiled to address concerns raised by academics and business leaders. Some tutors spend up to 70 per cent of their time correcting English; employers complain about job applications littered with errors.)

Once you have bought your reference books, they'll give you a feeling of satisfaction for many years – until they get out of date! An outlay of about £50 is all you need but you can spend as little as £30.00 and be fully equipped. To start with a good dictionary and the *New Oxford Dictionary for Writers and Editors* is the best recommendation I can make. (You can see how inconsistencies become annoying, when checking final proofs! You cannot have '£50' and '£30.00'. Use one or the other style but not both.)

The last key item is a bottle of Tippex (or similar) correction fluid. (Okay, if you want to be pedantic, it's

Tipp-ex.) This will quickly erase any alterations you have made that subsequently prove unwise, and it is better to use Tippex, which makes for neater presentation, rather than just cross out your corrections. Only use a correction fluid for your own marginal corrections you want to change. Never use it to cover the author's words. [This was done in the ancient past, and palimpsests were the result. That's not entirely true, of course, but at least I hope you will be encouraged to dig out a dictionary, if you need one.] A good subject knowledge is not necessary for general proofreading, but if you intend to specialise in medicine, for example, good medical dictionaries are essential.

CHAPTER 5

Spelling

Certain words seem to cause authors spelling problems. Once these have been noted and learnt, your ability to notice them with minimum effort improves dramatically. Here is a one-line test to check your spelling skills:

Unparalleled accomodation offerred for embarassed, harrassed comuters.

If you're excellent at spelling you'll have no problems. But don't worry if you're not 100 per cent proficient at it (very few people are). Your spelling will improve with practice, and a good dictionary (see Chapter 4) is essential if you are uncertain about certain word spellings such as, for example, *micro-organism, millennium, deoxyribonucleic acid, Ljubljana* (somewhere in Yugoslavia) or even if you think there might be two instead of three 'h's' in *Khrushchev*.

Nevertheless, it's fair to say that no one can expect to be a good proofreader unless they either know spellings well *or* recognise that they don't know. (**Note:** remember it's *either . . . or* but *neither . . . nor*.)

(**One-line test corrected:** Unparalleled accommodation offered for embarrassed, harassed commuters.)

A golden rule is always to check a word in your dictionary if you are in doubt about spelling accuracy. Where there are alternative ways of spelling a word, you can refer to the *New Oxford Dictionary for Writers and Editors* or any competent dictionary (see Chapter 4). Remember that the copy-editor who edited the typescript is not infallible, and that you will almost certainly pick up a few errors that were missed.

Most publishing houses have what are known as 'preferred spellings'. This means that certain word spellings are preferred as part of their 'house style'. Usually, the editor who sends you your proofs will send a list of preferred spellings (if any) so that you can follow the publisher's own particular style.

For example, Publisher A may prefer: *biassed, targetted, nonetheless, dispatch, mediaeval, encyclopaedia,* etc., whereas Publisher B may prefer: *biased, targeted, none the less* (three words), *despatch, medieval, encyclopedia,* etc. PS: one such list is given below.

Note: there is a perfect example of a typesetting error in the list that follows. Two entries have been transposed in error. Can you see which ones?

acknowledgement (not acknowledgment)
inquiry (for an investigation)
co-operate (not cooperate)
co-ordinate (not coordinate)
connection (not connexion)
despatch (not dispatch)
elite (no accent)
encyclopedia (not encyclopaedia)
enquiry (for a question)
focused (one 's')
further (not farther)
gram (not gramme)

inasmuch (one word)
appendices
in so far (three words)
judgement (not judgment)
medieval (not mediaeval)
nevertheless (one word)
none the less (three words)
premise (verb)
premiss (noun)
reflection
regime (no accent)
role (no accent)

There are of course many more (e.g. *by-law, centring, gypsy, guerilla, petty-bourgeois, storey* (of a house), *wagon,* etc. (The two entries on page 21 that need to be transposed are 'inquiry' and 'appendices'.) The copy-editor should have followed the preferred spellings, so when proofreading you will only have to check whether he/she has done so. However, on occasion you may be asked to leave minor points of style as they are, provided that the adopted mode of spelling is *consistent* throughout. (See also the section on **American Spellings** below.)

You will also meet the problem of 's' and 'z' spellings. Once again, the publisher's editor will let you know (usually you will see which anyway just by looking at the accompanying typescript or style sheet) whether the style is -ise or -ize. Publisher A may prefer 's' spellings: *organise, organisation*. Publisher B, however, may prefer -ize: *organize, organization*. The main thing is to be consistent.

Note: alternative spellings in quoted material, book and article titles should not be changed. Two quick examples: '. . . within which he also builds a high and very substantial stone Wall, with Battlements and Tarass round it, on the inside, with several Redouts and Half moones therein, after the manner of Fortifications.'

This quote is from a book, written in medieval times, describing the old buildings in the grounds of the Bishop's Palace in Wells, Somerset. Don't try to change punctuation, spelling, capitalisation, etc. It stays exactly as it is. (You can find a good example of original punctuation left unchanged in the prelims of this book, on the epigraph page – the quote from sonnet 129. The comma and em dash together induce apoplexy in today's copy-editor or proofreader.)

And if you saw a line from the Pussycat Dolls, don't try to change that either:

> When interviewed, she quoted from their song,
> looked blankly at the interviewer, purring,
> *'Doncha wish yo girlfriend was hot like me?'*

The rule about not changing original quotations seems to have affected the reproduction of some poems. Glancing at three randomly chosen examples of a William Blake quote actually gave three completely different versions in terms of capitalisation, comma use, and consistency. Here are two of them:

> *To see a World in a grain of sand*
> *And a Heaven in a wild flower,*
> *Hold Infinity in the palm of your hand*
> *And Eternity in an hour.*

> *To see a World in a Grain of Sand,*
> *And a Heaven in a Wild Flower,*
> *Hold Infinity in the palm of your hand,*
> *And Eternity in an hour.*

The following words must always be spelt -ise:

advertise	exercise
advise	improvise
analyse	incise
apprise	practise
arise	prise
catalyse	reprise
comprise	revise
compromise	supervise

despise	surmise
devise	surprise
disguise	televise
excise	treatise

Note the difference, of course, between *practise* (verb) and *practice* (noun). The verbs analyse and paralyse should always be spelt with 's' spellings, although they are spelt with a 'z' (analyze, paralyze) in **American Spellings** (see below). Etymologically, words of Latin or French derivation take -*ise*, those derived from Greek take -*ize*.

Other words you could add to the above are: chastise, circumcise, demise, enfranchise, enterprise, franchise, and merchandise.

Note: watch out carefully for these words: acco*mm*odate, ba*tt*alion, consensus, mille*nn*ium, supersede.

Here's a list of randomly chosen words to test your spelling skills (answers on page 28).

skullduggery	occured
achilles heel	skillfully
unco-operative	bougainvilla
gallopped	nightmareish
assertation	neice
self-same	participater
preempt	freize
liason	salutory
lambast	analagous
protecter	calender
satelite	caviarre
sieze	glutin
vigourous	sizable
absorbtion	plausable

seige   accessable
commitment   miniscule
innoculate   allright

5.1 American Spellings

Apart from instances (see above) of quoted material where the style of spelling must not be changed, occasionally you may be asked to 'anglicise' (or 'anglicize') proofs. [In case you're wondering why it's not 'Anglicise', where the word has been taken from the main noun, use lower case!] This simply means changing the American spellings to English ones, as well as changing words that have an American meaning into English. Normally the copy-editor will have been asked to do this, so the proofreader will just have to double-check. Sometimes the book might have been published already in hardback in the USA and a paperback edition could be planned for sale in the UK, so it must be made acceptable to the British reader. You should in any case be sent a list of spellings to watch out for, so don't worry if you are not absolutely familiar with them. Here's a short list of some better-known examples with their English/British equivalents:

behavior   behaviour
center   centre
check   cheque
color   colour
defense   defence
fiber   fibre
honor   honour
humor   humour
jeweler   jeweller
kilometer   kilometre

liter	litre
marvelous	marvellous
meter	metre
offense	offence
practice (noun & verb)	practise (verb)
tranquiliser	tranquilliser
traveler	traveller
whiskey	whisky*
woolen	woollen

(There are some words that are American and we probably use them without realising their origin: *blurb, commuter, gimmick, know-how, lifestyle, motel, stunt, teenager*, etc.)

The last point to note if you are asked to anglicise/ anglicize the spelling in a set of proofs is that you should also change those instances where Americans and British have different words for the same thing (as when we say *trainers*, Americans say *sneakers*.) For example:

USA	UK	USA	UK
apartment	flat	faucet	tap
baby carriage	pram	gasoline, gas	petrol
broiled meat	grilled	hood (of car)	bonnet
candy	sweets	instalment plan	hire purchase
cookie	biscuit	second floor	first floor
druggist	chemist	sidewalk (curb)	pavement (kerb)
elevator	lift	vacation	holiday
fall	autumn	windshield	windscreen

When anglicising proofs there are subtle differences that you need to know about. American publishers, for example, use double quotes and 'single within double', exactly the opposite of what is used in the UK (single quotes and 'double within single').

* 'Whisky' is Scottish but 'whiskey' is a whisky made in the US or Ireland.

Here are two examples:

UK: The reporter asked, 'What do you make of this "experiment" with Michael Jackson's face?'
US: The reporter asked, "What do you make of this 'experiment' with Michael Jackson's face?"

Also watch out for the full point (period) inside or outside closing quote marks:

UK: Turning into the sun, he began the long, winding drive through the cascades. He liked this country and felt unpressed, stopping now and then to make notes. . . about what he called 'memory snapshots'.
US: Turning into the sun, he began the long, winding drive through the cascades. He liked this country and felt unpressed, stopping now and then to make notes. . . about what he called "memory snapshots."

The list above is of course not exhaustive and there are also words that are the same but have a different meaning:

Word	USA meaning	UK meaning
bathe	take a bath	take a swim
bill	banknote	account, invoice
casket	coffin	lidded box
clippings	newspaper cuttings	hair trimmings
cord	electric flex	strong string
help	servant	aid
loafer	slip-on shoe	idler
private	public school	non-state school
raise	a rise	to lift

vest	waistcoat	undershirt
wash up	wash oneself	wash the dishes

In practice, you will not need to be familiar with all these and are unlikely, ever, to meet them in a single set of proofs that you have been asked to anglicise. However, it is best to be aware of them, and to be able to respond confidently when the subject arises.

Quick Spelling Test Answers

skulduggery	occurred
Achilles' heel	skilfully
uncooperative	bougainvillea
galloped	nightmarish
assertion	niece
selfsame (one word)	participator
pre-empt (hyphen)	frieze
liaison	salutary
lambaste	analogous
protector	calendar
satellite	caviar
seize	gluten
vigorous (but vigour)	sizeable
absorption	plausible
siege	accessible
commitment (but committed)	minuscule
inoculate	all right (two words)

Note: don't be alarmed if you didn't spot all the errors immediately, or even not at all. However, you should bear in mind that if you don't spot them, you are presuming the spelling is correct. It's only knowing a spelling might be wrong that makes someone check in a dictionary. The dictionary (include spellcheckers!) is there to help you; there is an answer for everything if you are prepared to look.

As a proofreader you'll be looking, among other things, for literals, misspellings in the text not noticed by the copy-editor (or even wrongly corrected by him/her!), or typographical errors, informally known as 'typos', typographical errors by the typesetter. It is a fact that probably over 99 per cent of the words in a set of proofs are correct. There will be a few needles in the haystack but, fortunately, the typos are usually glaringly obvious.

A momentary loss of concentration by the typesetter A momentary loss of concentration by the typesetter is not unusual (see above!). It is usually immediately noticeable if you are not hurrying to finish the work, and are practised in the skills of proofreading. As often as not it's a keyboard error as the finger slips over the wrong key. Let's look at that sentence again. as oftne ro not it's a-keyvoard error as the the finber slipps over the wrongh Key. There are ten errors. How many of them are immediately noticeable to you?

If it's your first set of proofs, you will want to make especially sure that you make them as error-free as possible; so don't have any qualms about reading them for a second time, just to ensure that nothing has been missed. It's always crucially important, either with your first set of proofs, or proofs from a new publisher, to do the work as professionally as possible. If it's done well, more proofs will be sent to you, and that means more cheques at the end of the month.

Talking of which, before moving on to the punctuation chapter, here is a chapter to awaken your interest more.

CHAPTER 6

Be motivated and be successful!

Let's imagine your first set of proofs has actually arrived by first-class post. You may have to sign for them if they have been sent by special delivery. Of course, you will already have been in contact by phone, fax or email with an editor. He/she will have described the nature of the book, its subject, length, and then asked if you are free to work on it.

Assuming you have agreed, you will have some idea of what to expect. With the proofs will be the corrected manuscript (in reality a typescript), which you must refer to in the course of proofreading. You may have been asked specifically to read against copy, that is, to follow word for word from the typescript. When you are starting out, this is absolutely essential, but more experienced proofreaders will not always need to read against copy. They will still turn over each page of the typescript as they read the proofs and a quick glance will alert them to any special instructions given by the copy-editor, so that they can make sure the typesetter has followed them. The more experienced proof-reader will thus have to refer only to the manuscript for guidance or where he/she is uncertain of any foreign words, spelling or terminology and wishes to check 'against copy'.

In many cases, you will be proofreading 'blind', that is without an edited typescript or manuscript. (This also applies to on-screen editing as nowadays fewer proof-readers work with 'hard copy'.) If this is the case, you need to be that little bit more careful.

Let's hope the first set of proofs is interesting. You could be reading just about anything. Here's a list of a number of books worked on by the author (and editor) of *The Pocket Book of Proofreading* over several months.

Inside Third World Cities	*Track Record*
Hampshire Cricketers	*Managerial Finance*
Occupation Nazi-Hunter	*Warriors of Rome*
In the Footsteps of Hannibal	*Origins of England*
Flash Gordon	*Santorini*
The Competitive Woman	*Travels with a 2CV*
Natural History Verse	*Sepulchre*
Guns and Goshawks	*Safer Driving*
Whirlwind	*Caspian Caviar*
Professional Services	*IT*
The Dancing Queen (Lola Montez)	*The Breed Woman*
Successful Sea Trout Angling	*The Bachman Books*
Victoria's Enemies (Military	*Stock Answers*
campaigns in the 19th century)	*Life of Madam Teresa*
Whose Health is it Anyway?	*Heatherlands*
The Natural History of Badgers	*Cloey: a True Story*
The Search for Extra-terrestrial	*Greek Cities*
Intelligence	*Finn's Travels*

Is there something in this diverse list that may have interested YOU? No special knowledge was needed for proofreading any of these titles. Over 30 titles from various publishers for which the lowest fee charged was £125, the highest £575, based on an average hourly rate (some years ago now) of between £12 to £15. This should give you the incentive to learn how it can be done. (Copy-editors can charge up to £20.00 [just a minute, shouldn't that be £20?] per hour, and much more for 'substantive' editing.)

Most freelances (if they are any good) usually have cheques outstanding (i.e. in the 'pipeline', awaiting payment) of over £2,000. The 180,000-plus books published annually in the United Kingdom provide the opportunity for plenty of copy-editing and proofreading work.

Note: one or two of the titles in the list on page 31 had been published before but in hardback. They were being 're-run' into paperback editions using a master disk. In effect, there was nothing to correct; one had to look only for the occasional computer glitch. This can be a frustrating experience, however. Reading 250 to 350 pages and finding nothing wrong at all, except half-way through the computer might have decided to start acting strangelyandthisis -disconcertxxx432ing (*sic*) to say the least! The consolation is that you are unlikely to be missing anything much at all, apart from that crazy glitch.

CHAPTER 7

Punctuation and some style points

The aim of punctuation is to make the sense of written words clear. It corresponds to the pauses and emphases in the spoken word. Today the guidelines are common sense and readability, and as a general rule it should be kept to a minimum. Unless asked, editors should not impose their own style on the copy and should use caution in any emendation. The subject is not as daunting as it might appear, and the 'Punctuation Queen', Lynne Truss, has got it sorted. There are certain conventions or rules to be followed, and when these are known, your task becomes that much easier.

The subject can be divided into the following sections:

full point; comma; semicolon; paragraphs; quotations; quotation marks; apostrophes; abbreviations and contractions; parentheses and brackets; dashes; hyphens; double punctuation; ellipses; numerals; dates; measurements; question marks and exclamations; capitalisation; time; money; foreign languages.

This book does not provide the most detailed guide possible to punctuation; for this, consult a reference book such as the *New Oxford Dictionary for Writers and Editors* or Fowler's *Modern English Usage*. It does provide, however, the basic rules that you must know if you are to proofread or copy-edit successfully. Other useful style arbiters include Gower's *Plain Words* and Partridge's *Usage and Abusage*.

It's a wise plan always to be on the lookout for newer, more recent editions of any reference books. The gamble is that you miss out on fantastic bargains in charity shops, like hardly used 900-page dictionaries for £1. The advice is to have the newest edition of just one or two books that count as your main reference books, but back these up with the bargains if you get the chance.

7.1 Full Point

There should be no full point (also known as full stop) at the end of items in a list of figures, plates, tables, etc. There may, however, be a full point at the end of 'displayed material', that is copy indented or otherwise made to stand out, in a list for example, from the main body of the text. A missing full point to be inserted in a manuscript or proof is shown thus: ⊙ (**See also:** double punctuation, parentheses, abbreviations and contractions.)

A full point is not used where a complete sentence is enclosed by parentheses within another sentence.

> Ms Anna Politkovskaya, an investigative journal-ist, was shot dead (it was President Putin's 54th birthday) in a lift outside her flat on Saturday, and protests over her murder quickly spread as far as Helsinki and America.

However, note the full point within parentheses in a complete, separate sentence.

> Byron died fighting for Greek independence. (He perished at Missolonghi, a town near the Gulf of Patras, in 1824.)

Contrast this with:

> Byron fell in love with the city of Athens (not altogether surprising).

7.2 Comma

Words such as *however, moreover,* are usually followed by a comma when used as the first word of a sentence; they are preceded and followed by a comma when used later in a sentence. For example:

> However, it was a chance not to be missed.
> They had, however, decided to accept the offer.

But note:

> However you look at it, it seems improbable.

In 'lists' of three or more items the comma should be omitted before the 'and' (also 'or'):

> Red, orange, yellow, green, blue, indigo and violet are the colours of the spectrum.
> Harry, James or George
> Claudia, Pamela and Naomi

A comma *not* omitted before 'and' in a list of three or more items is described as a serial (or list) comma (also known as the Oxford comma). This usage is common in the US. Be consistent: either include (Holly, Beatrice, and Rachel) or omit (Holly, Beatrice and Rachel).

Where two or more adjectives independently modify a noun, a comma should be used:

> a tall, reticulated giraffe
> a small, oblong table
> a huge, shiny, pink blancmange

However, where the second adjective and the noun are jointly modified by the first adjective, no comma is necessary:

> A short yellow minidress
> A large green monitor

Commas are often used instead of parentheses:

> These animals, make no mistake, must be fed twice a day.

Commas are not used with parenthetical dashes – they constitute sufficient pause:

> The volcano – often the subject of repeated warnings – erupted in September 2001.

A comma must not be used before the opening of parentheses:

> He signed a codicil (the first of many) to the will.

A comma is used before the introduction of quoted speech:

The scientist declared, 'Chimpanzees and early hominids [including Neanderthals] could have interbred.'

Note the following constructions:

The lead singer, Rupert Romaro, agreed to perform at the gig. 'Juicy', a hit for eleven weeks, was his first success. (Parenthetical nouns and phrases enclosed between commas.)

The singer Rupert Romaro agreed to perform. The hit 'Juicy' was Romaro's first success. (No commas required.)

The books included *Love Sonnets, Man and Superman*, and *Caught in the Net*. (Where one or more items in a 'list' contains 'and', a comma is used before the final 'and'.)

The books included *The Time Machine*; *Men, Women and Angels*; and *The Google Phenomenon*. (Here the rule is where one or more items in a list include a comma, use a semicolon to separate the items.)

that/which

That is the defining (or restrictive) pronoun. *Which* is the non-defining (or non-restrictive) pronoun. In general, when restrictive phrases are introduced, substitute *that* for *which*; thus a phrase beginning with *which* should always be set off by a comma.

The car that I like has wire wheels
The car, which I like very much, has wire wheels
(my liking of the car is incidental)

e.g./i.e./etc.

The rules are: e.g. – comma before
i.e. – comma before
etc. – comma before, if more than one term
precedes (e.g. nuts, raisins and almonds, etc.)
– comma after 'etc.' if followed by phrase
such as 'and so forth'.

7.3 Semicolon

A semicolon is stronger than a comma, but not as strong as a
full point. It is normally not used if followed by a conjunction.

Australian writers are not particularly prominent;
Australian poets are not even represented.

Australian writers are not particularly prominent,
but Australian poets are not even represented. (The
use of a conjunction reduces the semicolon to a
comma.)

If the sentences are not related use a full point rather than
semicolon:

Australian writers are not particularly prominent.
Australian kangaroos are hunted for food.

In a long series of a complicated nature, or with internal
punctuation, semicolons should be used for clarity:

The Eurovision Song Contest resulted in some high marks: France, 127; Greece, 128; Portugal, 126; Italy, 129; Switzerland, 130.

7.4 Colon

A colon is usually used to introduce a list, series or example (it should never be followed by a dash):

She lived for just three things: horses, horses and horses.

Use a colon after *as follows*, or *the following* if followed by enumerated items:

The procedure is as follows:
1. Place your right hand. . .

Fowler's *Modern English Usage* has a fine definition. Its function is: 'that of delivering the goods that have been invoiced in the preceding words'.

A colon is used between numbers in a statement of proportion (25:1); in biblical references (Gen. 2:5); and in digital/24-hour timekeeping (23:50).

It is also used by Americans starting a letter, as in:

Dear Mr. Ormsby-Gore:
Thank you for being such a good sport. . .

Note use of full point in Mr. as well. One of the strangest uses of the colon must be by Microsoft Word, combining it with a parenthesis to make a shortcut key for smiley faces, as in :(for ☹ and :) for ☺.

7.5 Paragraphs

Note how the modern style is normally to start a paragraph 'full out' or flush with the left-hand margin after a chapter opening (i.e. the first line) or after a subheading. All subsequent paragraphs are indented, usually by one *em* space (see section on dashes). An exception to note is where a quotation in the text is indented (displayed) – usually for quotations over 40 words or over 5 lines – the first line following the quotation may be full out if the sense and content are continued (i.e. a continuation of the paragraph containing the quote). Otherwise a new paragraph will be indented.

7.6 Quotations

Some publishers will stipulate that quotations over 40 words or over five lines are to be displayed. Others may state 60 words. This means that the quotation is indented (usually on both left and right) and is always separated from the main text by a line space above and below.

Note: proofreaders must always check spacing carefully, not just for quotations (i.e. that there is a one-line space above and below – not a two-line space, or none at all) but also the spacing above and below subheadings, chapter headings, in tables, between words, between lines, etc. Do not use quotation marks to mark the beginning and end of a quotation if the material is displayed. They are not necessary. If there are two (or more) closely related quotations, say, of 45, 25 and 35 words, all three may be displayed – as an exception to a general rule of 40 words or more. The copy-editor will use his or her own discretion, likewise if the quotation is 38 words or 44. The rule is not exact but approximate.

7.7 Quotation Marks

Generally, use single quotes except for a quotation within a quotation. (On a manuscript the copy-editor will usually write 'single quotes – double within single' in the margin so that the typesetter knows which style to follow. The instruction 'double quotes – single within double' is nowadays quite rare, except in the US where it is standard.)

Note: there is a good example of 'double within single' on the front cover, above the bear. The question mark goes outside the double closing quote, not being part of it, but inside the closing single quote. It's inside the quotation mark because the question mark is at the end of a complete sentence, beginning with a capital letter – the rule is the same as for a full point (see p. 34).

> She stated, 'This allegation of "loitering with
> intent" is without foundation.'
> The interviewer told him, 'Anyone who works at
> Google is a "googler" and the food is free.'

If the quotation contains a grammatically complete sentence starting with a capital letter, the full point precedes the closing quotation mark.

> Shelley said, 'Poets are the unacknowledged legis-
> lators of mankind.'
> He concluded that the company 'might decide to
> extend the franchise'.

Quotation marks may also be used with words and phrases that are given new, unfamiliar or slightly dubious meanings:

> She told me to take my 'etchings' elsewhere.
> Send me an email from your 'Blackberry'.

Note: The Blackberry [BlackBerry] device is too well known now to need quotation marks, unless for special emphasis, or effect, like sarcasm. Similarly, with this sentence: 'She [Eva Longoria] impressed me so much, I decided to google her in the morning.' Or: 'Do you like my new ring tone? Some guy just bluetoothed it to me.'

7.8 Apostrophes

An apostrophe is used to show possession. In English names and surnames use the possessive 's whenever possible: James's, St James's, Charles's, Strauss's. (Do spooks still meet in Brooks's?) It is usually omitted with di- and polysyllabic names, e.g. Charteris' book, also in French and Greek names.

For classical names use: Archimedes' principle, Mars', Venus', Jesus' disciples, Euripides' plays. There is no apostrophe in the following place names: All Souls, Earls Court, Golders Green, St Albans, St Ives.

Walk past a shop in any high street, and you'll often see misplaced apostrophes: pie's and burgers, tomato's, potatoe's, etc. – the 'grocer's apostrophe'!

An apostrophe can be used in plurals to avoid confusion, e.g. do's and don'ts (more correctly 'dos and don'ts'), p's and q's. Do not use it for plurals of capitalised abbreviations, e.g. BAs, CBEs, DVDs, MPs, STDs, UFOs, URLs, WMDs (note: the 1960s, the Joneses). There is also no apostrophe with: bus, flu, phone, fridge, thirties, plane, teens – although this is not for possession but for missing letters – and the apostrophe should strictly be kept in 'flu.

The apostrophe's misuse by the uneducated and its demise at the hands of large companies (who have excised it from brand names to simplify corporate logos, e.g. Harrods, Selfridges, Currys, etc.) is being monitored by the Apostrophe Protection Society, established to 'defend the punctuation mark's place in the English language'. (Top marks to Waterstone's for resisting the trend.)

Meanwhile, rogue apostrophes continue to pop up unexpectedly, as in this notice, spotted recently in a Tesco superstore: '£50-00 NOTE'S WILL NOT GO INTO THE SELF SERVICE TILL'S.' Apostrophes also frequently disappear, as in white van man's, 'HOWS MY DRIVING? PHONE 0800' etc.

7.9 Abbreviations and Contractions

It is important to distinguish between these. A contraction ends with the final letter of the word if spelt out in full (e.g. Dr - Doctor). An abbreviation (e.g.) does not, and therefore takes a full point(s). There are numerous exceptions (see, for example, the section on **Measurements**).

Whether abbreviations are used depends on the context: in formal or literary writing it is best to avoid using them, spelling out such abbreviations as e.g. (*exempli gratia*, for example) and i.e. (*id est*, that is). Scientific and technical works make extensive use of abbreviations.

Some abbreviations include:

e.g., i.e., fig., c. (*circa* [about]), *ibid.*, a.m., p.m., c.v., etc.

There should be no full points in sets of upper-case initials/acronyms:

ASBO, AWOL, BMA, DHSS, EEC, IVA, NATO, NGO, NSPCC, QC, RIP, RSPB, SME, UK, UNESCO, USA, USB, WLAN, etc.

Plural forms do not take 's except in lower-case initials:

Gordon wants to tax PDAs (personal digital assistants).
There were five MPs present at the meeting.
He handed me a dozen c.v.'s (or CVs).

The last example (c.v.'s) may (in some quarters) be stylistically 'correct' but it looks pretty horrible, and is therefore best avoided.

Whether full points are retained in B.A., M.A., Ph.D., B.Sc., etc. is a matter of the publisher's house-style. Note also that AD (*anno Domini* – in the year of the Lord) and BC (before Christ), as well as the compass points (N S E W; NNW; NNE, etc.) are usually set in small caps (capitals) as here, and you must write AD and BC in the correct way, i.e. AD precedes the date (AD 1066) and BC follows the date in question (55 BC). Note: third century AD; 5000 BC (no comma); 30,000 BC (comma with five or more digits). Where the comma goes in numbers is down to house style. Sometimes a thin space is used; this can now be marked on the proofs by a 'ball on a stick' (？).

A.M. (*ante meridiem* – before noon) and P.M. (*post meridiem* – after noon) are usually set in small caps but some publishers prefer lowercase (a.m. and p.m.). Also use small caps for BP, before the present (placed *after* the numerals).

Units of weight and measurement are always abbreviated in technical copy, without full points: mph, kph, cc, h, kw, ft, lb, etc. (See also contractions below.)

However, units should not be abbreviated following a number that is spelled out:

50 hp	fifty horsepower
15 MB	fifteen megabytes

Never begin a sentence with an abbreviation:

Number 10 Downing Street (not No.10...)

Large organisations, companies and government agencies frequently use their initials (e.g. ILO – International Labor Organization). The full name should always be spelled out, followed by the abbreviation in parentheses, when first used:

> The International Civil Aviation Organization (ICAO) is now a major influence in the movement towards greater airline safety. Not content with the manufacturer's claims for the Boeing 737, ICAO instigated this inquiry into...

Some contractions include:

> Mr, Mrs, Mlle, Dr, St (street or saint), cwt, ft, h, yd, Ltd, Mme

Note: n (note), f (folio), ff (following lines/pages), per cent, mph (miles per hour), km/h (kilometres per hour). No. or lower case no. always takes a full point – even though it is a contraction of *numero*.

In legal citations the name of a legal case, without citation numbers, is usually set in italics, with versus abbreviated to v. (with full point) set in roman (*Donoghue* v. *Stevenson*). (Lawyers always use 'and' for 'v' or 'versus' in speech; thus they will say: 'Donoghue and Stevenson'.)

7.10 Parentheses and Brackets

(   ) are known as parentheses. [   ] are called (square) brackets. The latter need not be used to avoid parentheses within parentheses, which are quite acceptable, e.g.

(See above for explanation (e.g. section 3) of terms.)

However, not *everyone* agrees with this. Just as publishers develop house styles and therefore preferences, some copy-editors and proofreaders prefer to avoid change in their most coveted conventions, though time has moved on. A good example of this is that there are extant copy-editors and proofreaders who bristle subconsciously at the sight of a split infinitive; their instinct is still to 'ambush' split infinitives, spearing them on the sharp points of their editing pens. **Note:** no comma *before* an opening parenthesis – with one exception – in a list in the text (e.g. I'd like (a) a new teddy, (b) a date with Eva, (c) an early night).

Square brackets are reserved for author's comments, interpolations, corrections, explanations, etc. in quotations that were not in the original text but have been added by authors, editors, etc. For example: She [Lola Montez] always wrote in the third person. **Note:** the consensus appears to be that parentheses-within-parentheses is the convention in the UK but that in US books, square brackets within parentheses are more usual. Incidentally, an odd use for parentheses has to be in some song titles, as in '(Is This the Way to) Amarillo?'

One last point to mention quickly is to distinguish between actual law cases quoted in textbooks and those mentioned in Law Reports in *The Times*, where you will *not* see a roman 'v' for versus (see pages 45–6). You'll also find paradigm examples of square brackets within parentheses! Here's one: *Campbell v MGN Ltd* ([2004] 2 AC 457). (There are said to be some 'wonderful square brackets' in Hansard, used for explanations.)

Square brackets are also used to 'fill in' parts of missing text, where word or words are added to make the sense or meaning clearer. Here is one rather ridiculously lengthy example to show that the 'and' added is not part of the original, as it's in square brackets:

> There are two moments in Lucretius' zoology that are notably Darwinian: the effect of organic adaptation and of domestication upon the preservation of the species; the survival value of swift legs, for instance, and of man's cooperation, both of which kept the earth stocked with animal life . . . [and] the Lucretian reiteration against teleology, that is, design in Nature, a favorite idea of Aristotle and of Lucretius' own much-scorned Stoics.

The ellipsis (see page 55) shows an omission, where the author chose to leave out part of the text of the quotation. The spelling of favourite as 'favorite' gives a clue that this is probably from a US text. I have no idea how the copy-editor is going to react to this example. It reminds me of a quote from Horace (see also page 129). 'I strive to be brief, and I become obscure.' I bet she'll get out her blue pen!

7.11 Dashes

It is important to distinguish between three sorts of dashes:

- the 'en' rule (–)
- the 'em' rule (—)
- the hyphen (-) (See the next section.)

The spaced en dash is used in parenthetical expressions normally set off with commas, particularly if the expression itself has commas, e.g.

> She cantered the horse – a fabulous, ex-circus one – for over an hour.

They are also used for afterthoughts or asides, indicating pauses in hesitant speech, etc.

> He caught the trout – a New Zealand record – on a mayfly nymph

or for interrupted or stuttering speech:

> 'She – she – she pretended not to know me when I stopped her on Fifth Avenue.'

If two en dashes appear in a sentence, the material before and after the parenthetical dashes must form a complete sentence. There should normally be no more than two en dashes in a sentence, although this rule can be suspended in dialogue.

The en rule is used for joining dates and ranges of numbers: 1914–18, 1998–99, chapters 3–5, pages 2–7. It is also used to join pairs where a hyphen is not used, etc.:

> The Sampras–Henman match
> The Winchester–Basingstoke–London route
> The hand–body relationship, space–time
> The Marxist–New Left split (Note Marxist-Leninist
> takes a hyphen as does Franco- in Franco-Prussian
> war as Franco- is a prefix that cannot stand alone.
> Similarly, Russo-Turkish war.)

Use an en rule to join such words where there is obviously no sense of unity or co-operation; if there is, use a hyphen.

The 'em' rule (—), so called because it represents the printer's measure equivalent to a lowercase 'm' in any given typeface, is used for parenthetical dashes. However, most UK publishers use a spaced en dash nowadays (as this book does, apart from the paragraph below!) for parenthetical pauses.

You will be able to see from the manuscript accompanying the proofs which measure the copy-editor has used. Pick up a book now and have a quick flip through the pages—you'll soon spot the different types of measures. Note how—in the US—em dashes are never spaced but always closed up. Em rules are 'the rule' in the US, the exception in the UK.

Note the following: the Lloyd-Smith talks (hyphen, one man); the Lloyd–Smith talks (en rule, two men); and the Lloyd-Smith–George affair (hyphen, en rule). The hyphen is smaller than the en rule, the en rule smaller than the em rule.

In a typed manuscript, a hyphen is used for an en dash, two hyphens for an em dash, an equal sign for a hyphen. The copy-editor marks up the various dashes for the printer before typesetting.

7.12 Hyphens

Be consistent in their use. If you have any doubt as to whether a word should be hyphenated or not, refer either to *New Hart's Rules* or the *New Oxford Dictionary for Writers and Editors*. The latter is really helpful for finding out quickly if a compound word is usually spelled as one word or hyphenated.

Authors often hyphenate words inconsistently, e.g. 'a ten year-old cathedral chorister'; 'a ten-year old cathedral chorister'; 'a ten-year-old cathedral chorister' (the last example is correct). 'Tricky' hyphens can surface in poetry too, as in 'dream-shadow-dim' (from James Elroy Flecker's 'Brumana') or 'Bloom-down-cheeked peaches' (from Christina Rossetti's 'Goblin Market').

Proofreaders and copy-editors can spend ages trying to figure out if an author, for example, really means 'modern-art installation' or 'modern art-installation' – or should they plump, and here's the quandary, for an opt out (often a cop-out), abandoning any idea for a hyphen, and leave as 'modern art installation'?

A proofreader must avoid equally the temptation to insert hyphens when not needed or to delete them when they should be left undisturbed. It takes practice to know when to use a hyphen – even for quite simple examples such as 'hero-worship', 'staging-post', 'jerry-built', or 'school-leaving age'.

Hyphens should be used to avoid any confusion in sense or meaning:

re-creation and recreation	re-cover and recover
re-count and recount	re-act and react
re-sign and resign	re-form and reform

A hyphen is used to separate identical vowels (but not in the US). Notice also the 'modern' tendency towards dispensing with the hyphen in words like 'coordinate' and 'cooperate' (so at least two of the examples below are on 'shaky' ground today).

pre-empt	re-echo	re-entry
co-ordinate	co-operation	anti-inflammatory

A hyphen is used to join a prefix to a proper name:

neo-Freudian	(but Neoplatonism)
anti-Labour	post-Darwinian

Note: Don't ever say that copy-editors don't have minds of their own! Oops, sorry, a double negative. (Sentences with double negatives are not just the preserve of careless writers, or chavs, as in, 'I ain't goin' nowhere.' They crop up with some regularity in Law Reports in *The Times*, such as this one: 'The fact that the circulation was wide could not lead to the conclusion that the Prince could not reasonably expect the contents of his journals to have been kept confidential.') First of all, you see when I came to check the proofs, the (most excellent) copy-editor had *excised* one of my examples, 'neo-Malthusian'. What was wrong with this I cannot say, other than perhaps there were already enough examples of 'neo-'. [This was the reason.] I rather like Malthus, although I haven't read any of his books. T.R. Malthus (1766–1834) was an English economist who developed a rather quaint theory. Supporters of his theory were known as 'Malthusians'. His idea was that increases in population tend to exceed increases in subsistence and that therefore sexual restraint should be exercised.

(Immediately I am thinking of Eva Longoria (see p. 42), and I don't think this is such a good idea! She's the diminutive but beautiful star of the TV comedy show *Desperate Housewives*, in case anyone still doesn't know. At 5′ 1″ she's only a little bigger than Archie. Don't the best things come in small parcels (proverb)? Eva opened the Harrods sale just after Christmas 2006. A *Daily Express* reporter said that to initiate the event she 'fittingly wore sky-high Christian Louboutin heels, a Dolce & Gabbana denim and PVC dress, and a cream Jasmine di Milo coat'. That's the kind of line that could easily sink any would-be proofreader, especially if devised as a test with traps by a wily publisher's editor. Eva called out to bargain hunters from a first-floor balcony: 'I hope you guys are ready to shop. . . Thank you for having me. This is actually my favourite department store.' Mohamed Al Fayed took her arm and they went on a walkabout, and I felt very jealous.)

Second of all, opposite 'but Neoplatonism' was a pencilled-in query for me to answer: *'Why?'* I have to say I don't know. I must have read it somewhere. This is only a 'pocket' book of proofreading. There's obviously a simple explanation as to why it should be 'neo-Malthusian' but 'Neoplatonism'. Possibly classical sources/names follow this convention? There's always so little time to find out. If you don't know the answer, or cannot find out from a quick trawl through your reference books, you might take some comfort, although it's not recommended, from the story below.

I can only ever remember one lesson from my RE teacher at school. In that lesson, the self-effacing reverend, whose face reflected a kind of sublime certainty and belief in God's goodness (a pre-Richard Dawkins era), spent forty-five minutes explaining that, if you didn't know the answer to a question – why the cosmos was so massively supersized, why older men can suddenly sprout wiry hairs on the ends of their noses, or even why it should be 'neo-Malthusian' but 'Neoplatonism' – it was perfectly acceptable to utter these three simple words, rich in dignity and humility: 'I don't know.' A bit like a religious cop-out really.

A hyphen is used to clarify the sense (although in modern usage, the first three examples make as much sense without the hyphen too):

> an ink-stained hand
> a well-known author
> a blood-red toe
> fluid-containing cells

It is also used to avoid repetition in such constructions as:

> a two- and three-pronged fork
> single- and double-breasted jackets
> the chapel-going mill- and factory-workers and
>   managers

and also for numbers (and fractions) when spelled out: twenty-one, two-thirds, and for line breaks at the end of a line of print: e.g.

philo-

sophical

and for certain verb-adverb combinations: paste-up, mark-up, blow-up. Hyphens are not used in adverb-adjective combinations where the meaning is clear: a beautifully designed patio; a richly decorated frieze. Note also the use of hyphens with adjectives:

in the long term	a long-term view
the upper classes	upper-class roles
the middle class	middle-class mores
grass roots	grass-roots antipathy

Many of the spelling problems that face an author or copy-editor are concerned with compound words, and when and where to hyphenate them. For instance, should you write *volleyball*, *volley-ball* or *volley ball*? The trend is towards spelling compound words as 'solid' or one word. If a modifier is formed in part by a noun, always hyphenate (e.g. spun-gold hair).

Note: compounds with better-, best-, little-, lesser-, well-, ill-, and so on are hyphenated when they precede the noun, unless the expression carries a modifier, in which case they are 'open'.

a well-known editor	*but* a very well known editor
an ill-tested hypothesis	*but* a notoriously ill tested hypothesis

Adverbs ending in -*ly* plus participle or adjective are not hyphenated (poorly seen, wholly invented, highly intricate, etc.).

7.13 Double Punctuation

Sometimes an author will use 'double' punctuation. The copy-editor should of course have corrected this. Nevertheless, it remains one of many minor points a proofreader needs to know. Some examples are: The girl replied, 'Is that the right way to treat a lady?'. Here the full point is superfluous. The question mark acts as a full point.

Similarly:

> He was the editor of *What iPod?*
> The article was published as 'The Limekilns, Beds.'

Note this exception: When is it correct to use the abbreviation *pp.*?
 Also, remember the rules of punctuation in parentheses:

> (He took with him blankets, sleeping bags,
>   provisions, etc.)
> He took with him various provisions (tea, coffee,
>   sugar, etc.).

7.14 Ellipses

Ellipses (singular: ellipsis) are used to show omissions in a quotation and take the form of three full points. Modern usage tends no longer to consider the addition of a fourth full point if the ellipsis occurs at the end of a sentence, so the rule normally is use three full points only. Always make sure the typesetter has spaced them properly (. . .). Quite often they will be too close together, or too far apart, or two points only, or . . , – all typesetting errors. A copy-editor will usually write in the margin of the copy '3-point spaced ellipses' in order to alert the typesetter to set them correctly and avoid...for example. They are not used at the beginning or end of a quotation unless required or necessary for sense. Some examples:

> If you go down to the woods today. . . a big
>   surprise (*This is for omission.*)
> He echoed the words of Goethe: 'What no man
>   knows alone could make us wise. . .'

7.15 Numerals

Whether you should use words or figures will depend very much on house style. In any event with your proofs should come a 'style sheet' (see later section) compiled by the copy-editor as a handy reference. This could be, for example, 'one to twelve spelled out – 13 upwards figures'. Or 'one to twenty spelled out – larger numbers expressed as figures'. An exception is when a series of numbers or lists of quantities would look 'wrong' if the style was adopted too literally, e.g. 'There were 25 hens, 175 eggs, 15 staff and five bags of grain.' Similarly, '3, 5, 7, 16, 23, and 102', etc. Figures are usually preferred for statistical or scientific material.

Use figures before abbreviations: 5 cwt, 9 lb (**NB:** not lbs). Use figures in percentages (15 per cent), except when starting a sentence. The usual rule is to spell out per cent but use % in tables or notes. (In some scientific books, the house style may specify exceptions, e.g. 'a 3% solution of sodium salts'.)

Remember that *any* number is spelled out if it begins a sentence, regardless of any inconsistency this may create:

> 25 litres of whisky were 'lifted' from the
> warehouse. (*wrong*)
> Twenty-five litres of whisky. . . (*correct*)

The copy-editor can also turn the sentence around in some way: A total of 25 litres of whisky. . .

Numbers should be spelled out in dialogue, unless this becomes exceptionally cumbersome. The copy-editor has not only to be consistent within a manuscript but also to be sensitive to different rules appropriate to different manuscripts. In a non-fiction text, for example, where there are frequent mentions of weights, measurements or distances, the copy-editor would probably choose to express these quantities always as figures, no matter how small their number, but in texts where there is only occasional mention of measurements, the copy-editor would choose to spell out: 'four miles' or 'twenty-seven degrees'.

The house style might state that numbers are to be elided (with the exception of measurements). This simply means: 25–9, 30–3, 98–9 and not 25–29, 30–33, 98–99. **Note:** 'teen' numbers are never elided; thus: 14–15, 16–19. BC dates cannot be elided either (29–24 BC).

Write 1,000 to 2,000 and not 1–2,000, which is ambiguous. Use 0.333 and not .333. Use figures to avoid too many hyphens, e.g. a 24-hour delay rather than a twenty-four-hour delay.

Remember to spell out 'round' numbers – so spell out figures that are 'about', as in the second example below, but this is not an unbreakable rule, as you'll see in example three! You can also use numerals for time (see page 69).

> Harrods sale attracted 5,201 customers in the first seven minutes.
> At least five thousand students perished in Tiananmen Square.
> A search for Google on www.google.com produces 2.7 billion hits – this is around 700 million more than for Microsoft.
> There are 101 million websites on the Internet (2006).

7.16 Dates

Simplify all dates by writing 1 June 2007 (not the many variants, such as 1st June, 2007; June 1st, 2007), without commas. After an exact date has been used, an elliptical reference to another date (in the same month) should be spelled out:

> On the 8 June the drought had lasted for seventy-eight days; on the ninth, violent thunderstorms unleashed a torrent of rain.

No comma is necessary when only the month and year are given:

> In September 1997 we grieved for our beloved princess, Diana, queen of our hearts.

For centuries (unless otherwise advised) spell out, lower case: the eighteenth century, the fifth century (not the 5th century/Century). Hyphenate when used adjectivally: seventeenth-century manuscripts (but in the seventeenth century). The style should be: 'in the mid-nineteenth century' (noun) but 'an early-tenth-century vase' (adjective).

Publishers do have different styles. In the example given above, another publisher may state:

> in the mid fifteenth century (no hyphen)
> mid-fifteenth-century art (two hyphens)

Note: the *New Oxford Dictionary for Writers and Editors* states that 'mid' generally forms open compounds, and as an example gives 'mid 17th century', noting that if used attributively – where an adjective precedes a noun (see p. 152) – you'll need a hyphen, as in 'mid-yellow teeth'. Compounds can be either open or solid, but as soon as I read about 'solid compounds', thinking them more to do with what's left over in the coffee machine, I close the grammar book quickly, and escape!

You'll remember from the section on **Numerals** (see above) that BC dates cannot be elided. However, some publishers prefer pairs of dates to be elided, thus: 1914–18, 1939–45, 1998–9.

Dates in chapter titles can be written 1976–77 (remember to be consistent throughout). An oblique stroke or solidus (/), known as a 'forward slash', is used to designate financial (US fiscal) years, e.g. 1929/30, 1998/9. You'll remember also (although this is more to do with copy-editing) to avoid beginning a sentence with a number: spell out or turn round.

Write 1980s, 1990s; from '1939 to 1945' rather than 'from 1939–45'; likewise 'between 1950 and 1956' rather than 'between 1950–1956'; '1 January to 12 March' rather than '1 January–12 March'. (Does this look odd to you: '2005s'? It's acceptable, as in: 'The Bordeaux négotiants were scooping up accolades for their 2005s.')

Distinguish between (note these are numerals and not dates):

    zero (0) and capital O
    Roman (I) and Arabic 1
    a British billion (million million) and an
    American billion (thousand million)

Millions and billions are best expressed as five million, twenty billion. However, use a figure in monetary sums: $5 billion.

7.17 Measurements

Adopt a consistent style throughout if abbreviations are used for yards, feet, inches, etc. (yd, ft, in). There are two main systems in common use: the imperial system and the metric or SI system. The latter system refers to the standard international units used in scientific and mathematical texts. The seven base units are as follows:

Physical Quantity	Name	Symbol/Abbrev.
Length	metre	m
Mass	kilogram	kg
Time	second	s
Electrical current	ampere	A
Thermodynamic temp.	kelvin	K
Amount of substance	mole	mol
Luminous intensity	candela	cd

Note that no full points are used in the abbreviations, and lower case is used except for those abbreviations derived from proper names. Unless you have a scientific background, however, it would be unwise to tackle such subjects to begin with. They require more concentrated effort than proofs of a more general nature.

Most people, unless they have specialised knowledge in these areas (medical books, for example), prefer straightforward reads to long lists of complicated calculations. The vast majority of general books will have only a few references (if any at all) to such things as feet, inches, kilograms or kilometres. ('The vast [pronounced as in 'massed'] majority' has lately become a vogue phrase, as well as a cliché, and seems particularly favoured by New Labour politicians and the BBC. Gordon Brown slightly morphed this phrase into 'mainstream opinion' in 2006.)

Remember the golden rule of consistency: avoid '15 m' on one page and '25 metres' the next.

7.18 Question Marks/Exclamation Marks

If the question mark (or interrogation point) forms part of the quoted material, it is placed inside the quotation marks:

> The examiner asked, 'Why have you failed to complete the question?'

Contrast this with a sentence where the question mark does not 'belong' with the quoted material:

> Why was Eve blushing when she said, 'I simply adore you'?

A similar rule applies with exclamation marks:

> The captain shouted, 'Fire on board!'
> How ridiculous [of Richard Hammond] to call this wreck a 'racing car'!

A question mark is not used with an indirect question:

> Nancy wondered why. She asked how old I was.

If a sentence is in reality a command, although in appearance interrogative, a full point replaces the question mark: Will you stop that noise. Requests or 'polite commands' take a question mark: Would you please answer this letter quickly? Remember that there is no full point after an exclamation mark.

7.19 Capitalisation

This subject has many pitfalls for the unwary. When to use an initial upper-case letter and when to use lower case will often be a test of a proofreader's skills. (As with hyphens, overuse is not recommended; because of the endless combinations of words an author can produce, correct hyphenation is a similar sort of challenge.) Read an early-nineteenth-century book and you may often find that words are capitalised almost at will – whenever the author decided, as if on a whim, that certain words should announce themselves as important by virtue of a capital letter. Fortunately, there are guidelines today that make the subject manageable.

We can invent a paragraph to illustrate the point:

> Wearing his Wellington boots, the Minister, who had only recently joined the Government, called in a whole panoply of Cabinet Ministers, Judges, Civil Servants and Hospital administrators, not to mention various Princes and a Regiment of Light Horse, as well as the King (who should have been in Church); and with a Roman sense of order, directed that they should accompany him on this Protean task to demonstrate that the Principles of Democratic Liberalism should be expounded North, South, East and West – in fact to every corner of the Empire.

How many capitals are correct/necessary? Strictly speaking there is in the above paragraph only one word (apart from the first) that needs capitalisation. Can you find out which one? Answer below. To return to the basic rule: avoid their overuse.

[Word that should be capitalised: Roman. You could also say Minister and King, as they are specific people in this paragraph.]

Here's another quick test, with the corrected text following:

> In 2003 professor Garamond returned to a more medical environment by taking the Chair of Clinical Chemistry in the university of Oxford.

> In 2003 Professor Garamond returned to a more medical environment by taking the chair of clinical chemistry in the University of Oxford.

Note: some proofreaders would keep the caps in 'Chair of Clinical Chemistry'. Much of this depends on context and other, usually minor and often subjective, variables (such as whether you read it in *The Times*, which I did, and so that's my excuse!).

You may sometimes be led to ponder over certain constructions when proofreading. For example, you might wonder about '*in* the University of Oxford' but it's quite correct. Probably it helps to know about such things as taking a chair, 'reading' a particular subject, being sent down, going up to, and coming down from university, etc., if only because you might find less to query! Generally, it's possible to work out the sense without having to query anything, although if working on a difficult text, for example in philosophy or medicine, it can be way too difficult to make sense of. Don't even try, there's no need; just look out for the usual errors you should have been trained to spot – literals, inconsistencies, editorial errors, layout mishaps, etc.

The state, government and politics

Use the state (the State, when a concept of political philosophy), state control, state monopoly. Use the

Government if referring to a particular body of persons, in an official sense, but adjectivally use government white paper; the House of Commons, House of Lords, the Senate (US); the Labour Party, the Conservative Party, Liberal, Socialist, etc., but use conservative, liberal, socialist, democratic, etc. when used adjectivally, and not as titles, of political parties.

Proper names

Use Leonardo da Vinci; the River Thames; Mother, Father when used in speech, as a form of address.

In religious texts, use Christianity, the Church of Rome, Islam, Marxism, the Catholic Church, the Church of England, the Church if the meaning refers to the Christian religion; use lower case for general senses, i.e. any church (building), an Anglo-Saxon church. Other examples: the Bible (but three bibles, biblical), God (the gods), Roman Catholic (catholic views, tastes), Puritan (puritanical).

Titles and ranks

Use Prime Minister Blair/Brown/Cameron, President Clinton, but the prime minister, president when referring to the office, the Communist party (Chinese communism); the King of Denmark (kings and queens in general sense), Pope Benedict XVI (Roman Catholic popes); the Minister of Defence, Professor of Medicine, Field Marshal, Major-General, Secretary-General, Lance-Corporal, Corporal, Sergeant, etc. (lower case if not used as title: Lance-Corporal Jones; a lance-corporal in the army); the Leader of the Opposition, the Duke of York, 'Sir Elton John takes David up the aisle', etc.

(The proofreader neatly encircled the initial capitals in 'Sir Elton John' and 'David' and quite correctly asked in the margin, 'Why would there be any query about caps here?' Answer: there isn't. I read the headline in the *Sun*, or the *Daily Express*, and it made me laugh. Doctors (like comedian Harry Hill who trained to be one) say we all need to laugh more! PS: I watched Dr Alice Roberts in her TV programme, *Don't Die Young*, and saw this useful quote: 'Take time to laugh – it is the music of the soul.' Sorry, no time to check in the reference book who said/wrote that.)

Adjectives/nouns derived from proper names

Capitals are used here, for example, Machiavellian (but chauvinism), venetian. If the connection over time has become remote, use lower case: wellington boot, protean, venetian blind, china clay, french window, etc.

Historical events/eras

the British Empire	the Roman Empire
the Renaissance	the space age
the Industrial Revolution	the Middle Ages
the Napoleonic Wars	the Dark Ages
the First World War	Byzantine

Trade names, names of aircraft, ships, railway engines

Concorde	SS (or S.S.) *South Seas*	Kleenex
Spitfire	MV *African Queen*	Bluetooth
Messerschmitt	HMS *Victory*	Mac
Queen Mary	Lindbergh's *Spirit of St Louis*	Windows
Tamagotchi	Netscape Navigator	Benylin

Geographical areas

In general use South America, West Germany, Northern Ireland, but northern Italy, southern Greece, the north of England (not recognised political or geographical divisions); Far Eastern, East Coast, but eastern for direction or locality; the Orient, but oriental (adjective) and Oriental (noun); the West; Western World; the Midwest; Midwesterner; western movies; the Continent (of Europe), but continental Europe, Gondwanaland, the Deep South, the South, southern, the earth, but Planet Earth, the Southern Cross, the Great Bear.

NB: Great Britain = England, Scotland and Wales
United Kingdom = Great Britain and Northern Ireland
British Isles = the United Kingdom and the Irish Republic [The proofreader asks, 'Out of interest, what do the Southern Irish call the islands?' It's a good question, one that results in a certain amount of head scratching.]
United States = North America
America (or the Americas) = North, South and Central America

Newspapers and journals/magazines

Newspaper titles are written in italics: the *Guardian*, the *Telegraph*, the *Daily News* (definite article, lower case roman), as are titles of journals and magazines: the *New Scientist*, *Jane's Defence Weekly*, *Hello!* Note the exceptions where the definite article is part of the title: *The Times*, *The Economist*, *The Bookseller*. Another exception is *The Independent*, which is as yet probably best left as the

Independent. (Does anyone remember the *Jyllands-Posten* newspaper in Denmark publishing twelve cartoons? The proofreader has told me twice, with a note in the margin, that this sentence is *irrelevant.* I know she's right but I'd like to let the irrelevancy stand. It's not about the cartoons, Muslims, freedom of speech, being sensitive towards the (religious) feelings of others. It's about my admiration for a remarkable woman, the Somali-born Ayaan Hirsi Ali, an articulate, brave woman. There's no real connection between the Danish newspaper and the former Dutch MP but when I see the name of the newspaper in print, a train of thought begins, and I remember listening to Ayaan speaking on the radio, and being impressed by her clarity and courage. Her story is told in a new book, *The Infidel: The Story of My Enlightenment,* published by Free Press (2007). I know this is just a little book about proofreading, so that's all.)

To provide a definitive synopsis of every possible example is simply impractical here. Nevertheless, the above guidelines will provide you with a sufficient framework of reference. Use common sense and caution, and if in doubt, refer to a work of reference (see section on **Reference Books**), such as the *New Oxford Dictionary for Writers and Editors* (*New ODWE*).

If the cartoon story above was about religion, law(s) and God, to demonstrate that it's always possible to find a (vaguely) apposite aphorism, here are three:

> It is the test of a good religion whether you can make a joke about it. (*Chesterton*)
> Where it is a duty to worship the sun it is pretty sure to be a crime to examine the laws of heat. (*Morley*)
> What makes God happy? Seeing a poor devil find a treasure and give it back. (*Yiddish proverb*)

Before ending this section, there's time to correct an error. Red herrings can lead you astray, and I've found a classic example of the value of up-to-date reference books.

My older edition of *ODWE* (1981) makes a big point that Rupert Murdoch's flagship newspaper should be written as *The Times*, with definite article '*The*' always being part of the title, cap and in italics. It also declares that the paper was established in 1788.

No mention is made of any other daily newspaper (as far as I can see). Fast forward to the *New Oxford Dictionary for Writers and Editors* (2005) and now there is mention of *The Guardian*, *The Independent*, and of course, *The Times* (the date it was established disappears), along with the *Daily Express*, the *Daily Mail*, and the *Daily Telegraph* ('the' lower case and roman). This must be a sign of some sort of democracy.

No mention is made of the *Daily Mirror*, the *Sun*, the *Star*, the *Sport*, or the *News of the World*. They're not important enough to figure! The editors must have calmly considered the inclusion of these newspapers, and given them the thumbs-down. *Not yet, old boy.*

Note how some of the previous statements in this section about newspaper titles are suddenly redundant.

Domain names

Watch out for correct capitalisation (or its absence) and anomalies in website domain names: YouTube, RightMove, eBay, Facebook, Yahoo!, ASOS, easyJet, MyTravel, etc. (*Ebay* occurs too, especially in some PC magazines.) This was spotted recently in *The Times*: 'EBay's sister site, eBay Express . . .' As it starts a sentence, you'd have to say it's correct. The Internet has given birth to *double* initial capitals!

Much depends on preferred usage by the company owning the domain name. Use (usually) lower case when the domain name/URL is quoted in full: e.g. www.johnlewis.com, www.timesonline.co.uk, www.amazon.com, www.myspace.com. (But: 'Have you posted your details on MySpace yet, bought a book from Amazon, or invested in a Second Life island or avatar?') Note that all domain names are case insensitive.

7.20 Time

Here are some examples:

> The office opens at 9.30 a.m.
> The surgery closes at 1500 hrs.
> It took John Lennon over nine months to complete the project.
> The Beatles left Abbey Road at half-past five.
> Martha Lane Fox had a two minutes' start (*but* one minute's start) over her competitors. (Note: a two-minute delay.)

7.21 Money

Pre-decimalisation (mega-rare nowadays!): express £, s, d (pounds, shillings and pence) as: £5 10s 4d (no full points). In a list, such as in a table, sums should be expressed as:

> £6.00 (not £6)   £8.00   £8.25   £0.50 (not 50p or .50p)

For occasional mention of a sum of pounds that can be expressed simply, spell out under 101 and even or 'round' hundreds:

seventy-five pounds
five thousand pounds
Google is capitalised at $120 billion and a fifth of
    its employees are millionaires.
A contribution of £289 was received for maintenance.

but 'The company's gross sales were £200 million with
£18 million profit after tax.'

Foreign currencies

Marks (DM) and francs (F): insert a space between letter
and figure, e.g. DM 25, 50 F, but dollar signs are close up,
as are euros: $25, €200.

7.22 Foreign Languages

Normally a foreign word or phrase is italicised if not in
common usage. If the word or phrase has become part of
everyday language it will normally be printed in roman
(i.e. upright) face. Some words that have become part of
the English language still retain their accents; this helps in
pronunciation (e.g. café, résumé, tête-à-tête).

Few publishers have definitive house styles regarding the
use of foreign words and phrases, but some do have clear
preferences – see appropriate house style guide. If in doubt,
follow the *New Oxford Dictionary for Writers and Editors*.

One famous American reference book, *Webster's
Ninth New Collegiate Dictionary* states: 'The decision as
to whether or not a word or phrase has been naturalized
in English will vary according to the subject matter and
the expected audience of the passage in which it appears.'

A list of foreign words and phrases in roman and italic,
as a general guide, follows in Chapter 8.

Words in roman and italic typefaces

Don't be apprehensive if you're unfamiliar with many of the words on the next few pages. Few people would be totally acquainted with all of them, and you would probably have to read hundreds of manuscripts before meeting every single example. If in doubt refer to a reference book, such as the *New Oxford Dictionary for Writers and Editors*, which should give you an instant explanation of the word or phrase as well as indicating whether it should be set in italic or roman typeface. (**NB:** the lists that follow represent the preference of *one* particular publisher only. The current trend is to set more and more words in roman rather than italic.)

Italics are used for book titles, paintings, drawings, sculptures, newspapers, magazines, long poems (e.g. *Paradise Lost*), to emphasise a word or phrase, for foreign words and phrases that haven't been adopted into the English language (though not for foreign proper names such as names of streets, places or organisations), plays, films, television (and radio) series (e.g. the *Richard & Judy* show), operas, ballet, scientific names (*Loxodonta africana*, African elephant), and for the names of vessels, aeroplanes, trains and spacecraft. Only the names of airplanes are italicised, not the type: Lindbergh's *Spirit of St Louis;* Boeing 747. Song titles, short poems, short stories and essays are usually in roman quoted – 'The Star-Spangled Banner'.

Note the roman 's' (possessive): '*Newsweek*'s contribution to reporting . . .' Always use roman for the possessive 's, when it follows a word in italic, unless it's part of a title, such as *New Hart's Rules*.

If a particularly unusual foreign word occurs many times in a single text, it is often italicised on first mention with a definition in roman, in parentheses, and thereafter set in roman. Commas, colons and semicolons *may* be set in the type (italic/bold/roman) of the preceding word. It might depend on whether the proofreader is sharp enough to notice.

Also use italics for letters mentioned by name (the letter *b*), and mathematical variables, whether in running text or display (let *x* equal. . .). When in doubt, it's preferable to leave roman. Italics should not be used for emphasis unless necessary for sense.

WORDS IN ROMAN TYPEFACE	
aide-de-camp	bourgeois (adj.)
al fresco	bourgeoisie (noun)
alias	bric-à-brac
apache	
apartheid	café
apropos	canard
attache	chargé d'affaires
aurora borealis	chiaroscuro
	cliché
billet-doux (pl. billets-doux)	clientele
bizarre	concierge
blitzkrieg	communiqué
bloc	consommé
bona fide	contretemps
bon vivant/viveur	cortège

crèche

crème fraîche

crêpe (Suzette) (de Chine)

cul-de-sac (pl. culs-de-sac)

cum

dèbâcle

debris

debutant(e)

denouement

de luxe

dilettante

doyen

dramatis personae

éclair

elite

émigré

entrée

entrepôt

entrepreneur

espresso

eau-de-Cologne

eau-de-vie

ex officio

façade

fashionista

fata morgana

fête

fiancé(e)

fleur-de-lis

fromage frais

gâteau

gendarme

genre

habeas corpus

hijab

hors-d'oeuvre

impasse

impresario

imprimateur

incommunicado

inamorato (fem. -a)

incognito

infra dig

lacuna

lingua franca

major-domo

matinée

mêlée

ménage

milieu

naive, naïve, naïf

naivety, naiveté, naïveté,

né(e)

niqab

op. cit.

papier mâché

parterre

parvenu

per annum

poste restante

post-mortem *or*

post mortem

prima facie

pro rata

protégé

recherché	terra firma
Reich	tête-à-tête
reveille	
rigor mortis	vade mecum
rissole	verbatim
role	versus
	via
sang froid	vice versa
sansculotte	viva voce
sauerkraut	
soirée	wagon-lit
soufflé	
soupçon	yashmak
subpoena	

WORDS IN ITALIC TYPEFACE

ad hoc	*belles-lettres*
ad nauseam	*bête noire*
ad valorem	*bijou (pl. -x)*
aficionado	*bon gout*
amour propre	*bonhomie*
ancien régime	*bon mot (pl. bon mots)*
angst	*brouhaha*
a posteriori	
a priori	*c., circa (about)*
au fait	*cappuccino*
au fond	*carte blanche*
au revoir	*casus belli*
auf Wiedersehen	*caveat emptor*
au gratin	*cognoscente*
	coup de grâce
badinage	*coup de pied*
beaux-arts	*coup d'état*
belle époque	*coup de théâtre*

court bouillon
crime passionnel
curriculum vitae

décolletage
de facto
déjà vu
de jure
demi-monde
demi-tasse
de rigueur
déshabillé
Deus ex machina
Dieu et mon droit
dolce vita
douane
double entendre

élan
en bloc
en masse
en passant
en route
entente cordiale
ex cathedra

fait accompli
faute de mieux
faux pas
felo de se
femme fatale
fille de joie
fin de siècle

gamine
garçon
grand monde
gravitas

hara-kiri
haute couture/cuisine
honi soit qui mal y pense
hors de combat

ibidem (abbr. ibid.)
ingénue
in utero
in situ
in vitro
in vivo

jeu d'esprit
juste milieu

laissez-faire
lèse-majesté

mens rea
mise en scène
modus operandi
modus vivendi

ne plus ultra
nil desperandum
noblesse oblige
nolens volens
nom de plume
non sequitur

pace
par excellence
passim
per se
petit four (pl. petits fours)
pièce de résistance
pied-à-terre
pro tempore
putsch

raison d'être	*sub rosa*
rapprochement	*sui generis*
realpolitik	*sympathique*
rechauffé (fem. -ée)	
retroussé (fem. -ée)	*tabula rasa*
risqué	*terra incognito*
	tour de force
samurai	*tu quoque!*
sangria	*trompe-l'oeil*
sans souci	
savant (fem. -e)	*ultra vires*
savoir-faire	
schadenfreude	*vendeuse*
señor	*verboten*
simpatico	*vers libre*
sine anno	*vide*
sine die	*vis-à-vis*
sine qua non	*volte face*
son et lumière	
sotto voce	*Wehrmacht*
status quo	*Weltschmerz*
status quo ante	
Sturm und Drang	*Zollverein*
sub judice	

Lists like those above can't be exhaustive – without turning this little pocketbook into a dictionary. It's more house style, a particular publisher's preference, than current usage. There's no mention, for example, of brio, chutzpah, pommes frites or *beau geste, chambré, pis aller, sprezzatura, ultima Thule, umma* (also *ummah*)!

Any italicised word *must* carry accents if it has one (or more), although words in roman are often excused them. Lese-majesty is a good example. The *New Oxford Dictionary for Writers and Editors* (*New ODWE*) prefers it like that (roman, no accents). Compare with the non-anglicised, original French: *lèse-majesté*. More foreign words are now anglicised than ever before. It's usual, for example, to see sotto voce in roman today whereas a few years ago, it was more *sotto voce*. It's as if the English language is so powerful that it assumes to itself usage of foreign words. It assimilates and conquers fairly effortlessly.

I did mention in the *Preface* that proofreading and copy-editing will teach you fresh ways of looking at words. I forgot about all the *new* words you can learn when proofreading esoteric typescripts or 'chav' auto-biographies – you'll be kept on your toes. These are three favourites: *muffin top* – the flabby bit of waist, or midriff, hanging out between a woman's trousers and her top; *google drift* – starting out looking for something in a web search and finding something else; and *smirting* – flirting with someone while having a fag outside the office.

Being a good proofreader is not unlike being a prince (or princess) of Serendip – those three princes famous for the gift of making fortunate discoveries by chance or accident. Training is supposed to make the searching and finding less like chance or accident. Although you are looking for tiny errors, the simple and sometimes tedious process of discovering them can be satisfying, as well as the journey you take while looking.

Searching for one thing frequently leads to another. You could, for example, be checking the spelling of 'Higgs boson', a very rare particle that lots of scientists are looking for and none has yet managed to find, and then stumble across a new word, 'Plutoed', chosen by the American Dialect Society as its (2006) word of the year, after Pluto lost its status as a planet. It means to demote or devalue. [It is rumoured in the blogosphere that scientists may already have glimpsed the Higgs particle, aka the God particle, thought to give everything in the universe its mass (*New Scientist*, 'Glimpses of the God particle', 3 March 2007, pp. 8–11).]

Before long you could be leafing through a reference book to see if the quote from a tomb inscription relates to Queen Nefertari or Queen Nefertiti. Actually, it's the former, and here's the quote anyway because it's still beautiful after 3,000 years. According to research led by Devandra Singh of the University of Texas at Austin, a narrow waist in women equals health, fertility and desirability. The favourite queen of King Rameses II, Queen Nefertari, was even described in this way:

> My love is unique; no one can rival her, for she is the most beautiful woman alive. . . She radiates perfection and glows with health. The glance of her eye is gorgeous. . . Long-necked and milky breasted she is, her hair the colour of pure lapis. Gold is nothing compared to her arms, and her fingers are like lotus flowers. Her buttocks are full, but her waist is narrow. As for her thighs – they only add to her beauty. . . Just by passing, she has stolen away my heart.

At least it makes up for the work you might be doing on economic quartiles, canine obesity, or how unleashing hamster power could be an environmentally friendly answer to the impending energy crisis . . .

CHAPTER 9

A note on headings

If a manuscript or typescript has headings, the author and/or copy-editor will have marked these in a certain way in order to distinguish them according to their 'weight' or value. If the chapter heading is to be an 'A' heading, there will not normally be more than three or four types or levels of heading (B, C, D and E), in descending order of importance, so as not to confuse the reader. (**Note:** no full point after headings.)

Headings are normally set flush with the left-hand margin, with a one-line space (or two-line space) above and one below, but in any event whether headings are centred or 'ranged left/flush left' will be a matter for the designer. After A, B and C headings the text is usually 'full out', i.e. flush with the left-hand margin, not indented as for a paragraph.

Modern practice is not to number headings, except in either STM (scientific, technical and medical) books or unless essential for some other reason, i.e. the layout of the text. (I guess I am not so modern; the copy-editor reminded me with a 'but *you* do!' in the margin – so *mea culpa*.)

Here are some examples of headings:

THE ECO TRAVEL INDUSTRY IN BRITAIN TODAY
('A' heading)

The Long-term Consequences of Cheaper Air Travel
('B' heading)

Air Travel in Europe
('C' heading)

European competition. With the advent of the European Economic Community, competition rules in the member states . . .
('D' heading)

This is just one particular style. There are many variations but as a proofreader, you will only have to see that the appropriate headings are consistent, and follow the appropriate style.

Résumé

We have now covered much of the essential knowledge that you need to acquire in order to proofread (or copy-edit) successfully. Before beginning Chapter 19 on **Getting Started,** there are a few further points to consider. These are:

- the system of numbered notes used in bibliographical references;
- the system known as the Harvard system in bibliographical references;
- the layout of a list of references;
- the layout of a bibliography;
- tables and figures with examples;
- the index, and
- marks used in correcting proofs.

CHAPTER 10

References and notes

Many sets of proofs will of course contain no notes or references at all. These proofs are much more straightforward but, depending on the type of work available, a proofreader needs to be familiar with these systems. Some authors (fortunately) are just *so* meticulous, presenting the copy-editor with near faultless typescripts; and this can result in proofs so 'clean' that it may be hard to find any errors. You'll see from such typescripts how little work the copy-editor has had to do, as regards corrections.

Once you have read through several books with notes or references, you will soon recognise the styles used, and will be able to notice minor inconsistencies with surprising ease. As usual, different publishers have different styles, and there are many variations and modifications of the basic forms in use throughout the academic disciplines and various speciality fields. It's all about the systems used to set out information about sources. Here are three examples:

Smith, J.H. (2007) *Lions of the Serengeti*, Routledge & Kegan Paul, London, pp. 21–2.

Smith, J.H. *Lions of the Serengeti* (Routledge & Kegan Paul, London, 2007), pp. 21–2.

Smith, J.H. (2007), *Lions of the Serengeti* (London: Routledge & Kegan Paul), pp. 21–2.

There are several different 'variations on a theme'. Fortunately, there are established styles and/or conventions for the citation of sources, such as the numbered note system (e.g. Vancouver system) and the Harvard system of referencing.

Note: if the book has been co-authored or multi-authored, check that the copy-editors and authors have adopted a consistent style throughout (e.g. used the same spellings, heading layout, etc.), unless otherwise instructed. Remember that the copy-editor should have done this already, so it is just a case of reading and being aware of the style at the same time.

In terms of consistency, be aware that little things often get missed: the full stop at the end of a reference, the use of colon or semicolon in references (or not, as style dictates). Look out for 'crafty' style variations: distinctive punctuation, compressed (i.e. lack of) spacing (e.g. between dates, journal numbers, page numbers), use of italics, etc.

10.1 Numbered Note System (e.g. Vancouver System)

The numbered note system of references is often used for social science, medical and humanities books. In one form, it's known as the Vancouver System, ever since a group of editors sat round a big table in Vancouver and decided on the eponymous name after a group meeting. Parenthetical or superscript numbers are used in the text of the paper or book, which match a numbered list of sources at the end. Exact formats vary, which is another way of saying that the mix of disciplines, publishers, and editors hardly ever leads to consensus in citation styles.

The references will probably have been placed at the end of each chapter, but occasionally they will be found together at the end of the book. In each chapter the references are numbered sequentially with superscripts in the appropriate place ([1], [12], [24]) etc. The superscript number can only be used once in each chapter, so if two or more references are intended to the same note, new numbers must be used. (The copy-editor lightly disagreed with me at this point, pointing out that styles do differ. The same number can in fact often be repeated, referring to the same note.)

> Smith and Watson[1] have described the process by which the extraction of high-grade silver ore[2] can be realised without the use of expensive equipment as described by Moriarty.[3]

Note that the punctuation precedes the superscript number – with the exception of the dash. When checking proofs all you have to do is to see that they are numbered consecutively, and that none has been omitted.

The notes or references at the end of each chapter have a definite style – you will see from the proofs which has been followed – and you should note the difference in style between notes or footnotes and a list of references or bibliography.

Here is an example of the numbered note system. The superscript numbers appear in the appropriate place(s) in the text, signalling footnotes or 'endnotes', usually followed by a bibliography. (Footnotes appear at the bottom of a page; endnotes at the end of a chapter or book. Some publications use footnotes for a dual purpose: a) to give the full citation of a source; and b) to make 'tangential' comments of interest to the reader. The idea of placing a footnote at the bottom of the page, when making some sort of passing or tangential reference [i.e. to a bear[1]] is so that it doesn't detract from the main point, which it might if 'embedded' in the text. Other publications use the *Harvard style or system* of notation for sources, and footnotes just for points of interest or information.)

1. W.S. Churchill, *My Early Life*, 1st edn (Longman, Green and Co., London, 1924), vol. 3, pp. 99–101.
2. F.M.S. Grouse and C. Kennedy, *One For The Road* (Thomas Nelson and Sons, Edinburgh, 2007), p. 50.
3. J. Moriarty, *Sherlock Holmes in London* (Crime Publishing Inc., New York, 1974), pp. 21–2.
4. A. Litvinenko, *Polonium-210 Used by FSB to Hide the Truth?* (Campaigning Books, London, 2007), p. 24.

Notes can be in different formats.

1. Hardy, *The Early Life*, 132
2. Ibid., 76
3. Gibbon, *Decline and Fall*, iii, 425 (ch. xxxvii).
4. Op. cit., ii, 580 (ch. xvi).

('Ibid.' here means 'in the same place', i.e. referring to the same source or book (*The Early Life*). Ibid. is normally used when a note refers back to the same source as the note preceding it; thus only the page number may change. The word 'ibid.' is set in roman, followed by a comma,

---

[1]Archibald Ormsby-Gore was last seen clutched in the arms of Sir John Betjeman as the poet lay dying on a bed in Cornwall.

and the page number. 'Op. cit.' here means 'in the work cited' or 'in the same work' (*Decline and Fall*), but vol. ii rather than vol. iii. Ibid., loc. cit., op. cit. and other Latin abbreviations are used in notes, especially in classical texts, to help simplify the notes! Ibid., for example, is a way of indicating the same source as quoted immediately before. It saves time and space.)

1. L. Toulmin Smith (ed.), *Leland's Itinerary in England and Wales* (1964) vol. I, p. 93.
2. Eton MS 213 fo. 230v. Translation by Peter Thorburn.
3. *The Age of Chivalry* (catalogue), Royal Academy of Arts (1987), 481–2.
4. *Ibid.*, 307.

If you look closely, you'll see minor differences in style, e.g. ibid. may, or may not be, in italics. It can be easy to panic when confronted by pages of notes and/or references, especially when the style seems unfamiliar, if not alien, and you have no idea what some arcane and thoroughly mysterious lines, such as this one, mean:

HMC *Wells* I, 59; *Liber Albus* I fo. 50d.

Don't worry! The copy-editor might have had to sweat a little but as the proofreader, you need only look out for inconsistencies and the more obvious errors.

American Styles for Book References

American publishers, as you might expect, have different ideas. For example, references for books may look as follows:

(one author)
> 1. James D. Smith, *Tsunami Countdown* (New York: Harper & Row, 2005), 121–4.

(two authors)
> 2. Robert Bloomfield and Patricia Greenfield, *Language And Style* (New York: Academic Press, 1999), 90.

(three authors)
> 3. David R. Hall, John D. Donaldson, and Melvin E. Kaye, *The Mentality of Apes* (New Haven, Connecticut: Yale University Press, 2004), 24–6.

(more than three)
> 3. George Edwards *et al.*, *Excessive Cognitive Development* (Florida: Lake Westbound Press, 1997), 50. (In medical works, when the Vancouver system is used, the names of up to six authors are used; if the number is seven or more, the reference will mention the first three, then it's *et al.*)

Other variations are numerous:

> 32. James D. Smith, *Tsunami Countdown*, Harper & Row, New York, 1980, pp. 121–4.

or

> 32. James D. Smith (1980), *Tsunami Countdown* (New York: Harper & Row), pp. 121–4.

References for Articles and Journals

> 1. James W. Nelson, "The Role of Women in Autocratic Societies," *History Journal* 97 (1994): 720
> 2. Walter Kline, "The Election of President Clinton," *Time Magazine*, 14 May 1990, 15–19.

Note the double quotes, as this is a US publication. [Here's a strange observation: if sending a letter to *The Times*, the house style is double quotes, single within double – except they'll do the setting for you, so there's no need to follow this slavishly!]

Notes may be ranged right/justified too. Here's the Churchill note or reference again (see page 84) with a few deliberate mistakes:

> 1. W.S,Churchill. *My early Life,* 1sr Ed. (Longman- Green & Co,London, 1925; Vol.3, p.99-101.

Note that the spacing is wrong in a few places. Published titles should be in initial upper case in italics. Ed. usually refers to Editor/Edited; edn (a contraction) to edition; volume can be either Vol. or vol. (but not both!). This is a matter of house style, as is the question of whether the notes begin W.S. Smith or Smith, W.S. In medical journals, you might see: Smith J.W. (1990) Bla bla (article title). *Lancet* **1**:2–4. No quotes and volume number in bold.

Note: subsequent references to a book in the notes of each section, if given in full, would be fairly repetitive. A shortened version can therefore be used, where a 'short title' of the book is given together with basic details (which may, or may not, include the author's initials):

> 29. Churchill, *My Early Life*, vol. 3, pp. 89–90.

Abbreviations for volume and page numbers (especially in the US), if occurring together, are often omitted, with no space following the colon:

> 29. Churchill, *My Early Life*, 3:89–90.

Have a look at this construction:

> 1. T.S. Jones, 'Running a flight-test on Concorde'
> in R.S. Day (ed.), *Guide to Aviation History*
> (Flight Publishing, London, 1988), p. 35.

Notice that the article/chapter title begins with an initial capital in the first word. This is not obligatory – just one particular style. It could equally be 'Running a Flight-test on Concorde'. Subsequent references can also be abbreviated: 1. Jones, Concorde, p. 53; or 1. Jones, 'Running a Flight-test', p. 53.

Periodicals
> 36. Gordon Rivers, 'Hindu Cults', *Anthropological Review*, Vol. XXIV (1955), pp. 175–9.

Unpublished works
> 37. George K. Newman, 'Prehistoric Reptiles'.
> Ph.D. Thesis, Harvard University, 1991.

Newspapers
> 38. Katrina Harper, 'Manhattan Penthouse at $US100,000 a Month', *Washington Post*, 18 January 2003.

A direct reference to a newspaper will give only the title of the newspaper and the date:

39. *Observer*, 2 May 2007 (no need for definite article).

A more detailed reference to a newspaper article (as in reference 38 above) might be:

> 40. Courtney Love, 'Getting Arrested for an Air-
> rage Incident on a Virgin Atlantic Flight',
> *Observer*, 2 May 2006.

If no date is available for a publication, you may see the abbreviation 'n.d.' (no date).

Plays

> 1. *Much Ado About Nothing*, Act 2 Scene 1   *or*
> 2. *All's Well That Ends Well*, act 4, sc. 1, lines 12–14.

10.2 The Harvard System

This system, using parenthetical references (also known as the author–date system), is often used in scientific, technical and medical (STM) books. The Harvard system is actually the most commonly used reference method, especially in the physical and social sciences. No superscript numbers are used; instead the author's name is given in the text (surname only) together with the year of publication and a page reference, if any.

> . . . and the formal procedure known as plea bargaining (Williams, 1989, p. 24) was developed . . .

Another form is: (Williams, 1989:24), or (Williams 1989, 24). If the author's name is referred to in the text, the reference will be . . . plea bargaining initiated by Williams (1989, 24) or if there is no page reference, just: Williams (1989).

Where the author has published two or more books in the same year, the correct reference will be:

> Williams (1998a, 1998b)

in the case of two works. If there are two or three authors: (Todd and Meredith 1989); (Todd, Meredith and Hardy

1989). If more than three authors: (Todd *et al.* 1989), with the first mention of the reference given in full. Consistency in the style adopted is often better than adhering too rigidly to a set of house-style rules – but be warned, you will get no thanks from the publisher for your 'correcting', if involving vast costs!

Bibliography

A bibliography gives a complete list of all the works that have been cited in the text or notes, and is always given alphabetically, without any numbering.

If the Harvard system is adopted, the references to which the text or parenthetical references refer will appear listed at the end of the book, immediately before the index.

The volume number of a journal title may be in either italics or bold, followed by the page numbers in roman face. In some instances both vol. (volume) and p. (page) or pp. (pages) can be dispensed with, but if there is no volume number, it will be necessary to add p. or pp. before the relevant page number(s), as can be seen below in the examples:

Schaller, G. (1977) 'The declining habitat of the Cameroon green monkey'. *Animal Behaviour*, 24: 120–5.
Sheridan, K. (1998) 'Plumed birds of paradise in New Guinea'. *Exotic Zoology*, pp. 2–3.
Stephens, G.S. (2006) *Breeding Rare Animals in Zoos.* ABA Publishing, West Carolina, p. 42.

Never be too concerned if the style you have to follow is an unfamiliar one. If in doubt, you can always ask to be sent a book that has already been published, and which follows the same style in terms of references or notes. This should clarify matters in a few minutes. In any event the copy-editor should have made all the necessary changes and you will only be looking for the typesetter's occasional 'typo'. These typos are getting increasingly rare, like exotic animals. This is because most books are copy-edited on-screen, so any errors are the author's (and not picked up) or the copy-editor's added in!

10.3 Further Reading Lists

A select bibliography or reading list will not record all the works cited, but instead lists the major sources.

Colchester, L.S. (1997) 'Notes on Wells Cathedral and the Bishop's Palace', *Ecclesiastical News*, vol. 9, pp. 12–17

Granger, F. (1997) *Proposals for Anglo-Greek Development*, 3rd edn, Financial Press, London

Horsham, C.H. (1992) *An Educational Blueprint for Gifted Children*, Bluecoat Publications, London

Lanz, E.M. (1995) 'Physical education in primary schools', unpublished PhD thesis, University of Wales

Latham, W. and Bain, J. (1996) *Studies in Musical Composition*, Purcell Press, Harrow, p. 27

Ritchie, G. (2007) *The Prefect System in Private Schools*, Southover Press, Wells, p. 24

Tadiq, M. (2005) 'Why Ayaan Hirsi Ali is a True Heroine', *Liberal Views Magazine,* vol. 2, p. 15

Note: if two or more authors are cited, ensure consistency with the use of 'and' or '&'.

There are different ways of setting out a biblio-graphical list. Exact formats vary. Perhaps you've heard that somewhere before! For example, you can have the second (and any subsequent) line(s) of a reference (known as 'turnovers') ranged left and the reference spaced rather than indented. It depends on house style (as does depth of indent).

Colchester, L.S. (1997) 'Notes on Wells Cathedral and the Bishop's Palace', *Ecclestiastical News*, vol. 9, pp. 12–17

Murino, Caterina (2007) 'Playing Solange in the 21st Bond Movie', *Film Review*, vol. xxv, p. 19–21

Notice that PhD (Doctor of Philosophy) is often used in the UK. Compare with reference 37 on page 88 where (in the US) full stops are normally used (Ph.D.)

If two or more works are cited by the same author, they should be listed in chronological order, and the author's name for the second and subsequent works can be replaced by a rule – usually one of 2 (sometimes 3) ems. Thus:

Stubbs, W.N. (1995) *Flying Solo in India*, ATM Press, Truro
——(2001) BOAC and Overseas Air-routes, CUP, Cambridge
——(2002) *A Squadron Leader's Memoirs*, Nelson, London

A rule of 2 ems is acceptable. Three ems is considered an old-fashioned style.

Just briefly, be aware of differing styles, as in these examples:

Gibbon, Edward, *A Vindication of some Passages in the Fifteenth and Seventeenth Chapters of the History of the Decline and Fall of the Roman Empire*, with a preface by H.R. Trevor-Roper, Oxford University Press, 1961

———*Autobiography* (edited Lord Sheffield), Oxford University Press, 1954

This style seems 'hot' on colons:

Crawford, M.H.: *The Roman Republic* (1978, Glasgow)
———: *Coinage and Money under the Roman Republic* (1985, London)

10.4 Electronic Sources

Authors need to find standardised ways to refer to electronic sources such as Internet documents, videos, email messages, film on laser disc, web pages, URLs/ HTML links, articles in online journals, scientific papers, etc. Not surprisingly, different disciplines use different types of electronic sources.

Copy-editors and proofreaders should be pleased (as long as authors know how to use them!) with the advent of several software programs that can produce citation records in a range of approved citation formats – including the ever-popular Harvard system.

If listing a web page as a source, authors should include the date when they accessed/read the page (as well as the URL). This allows the reader to judge if he or she is seeing/reading the same version of the web page being looked at.

CHAPTER 11

Figures and tables

11.1 Figures

Figures, like tables, are usually 'keyed in' by chapter, e.g. Figure 2.1, Figure 2.2, etc. (**Note:** always ensure that the use of either 'Fig.' or 'Figure' is consistent.) The author or copy-editor will have marked in the margin of the typescript the approximate location(s) of the figures, e.g. (Insert Fig. 2.2 about here) or keyed/tagged it into the on-screen file.

The proofreader has to check that the figures have reproduced clearly and that the use of upper/lower case for the figure captions matches that used in the text.

The copy-editor will also insert the figures in their appropriate locations, making sure to number the page, e.g. if Figure 2.5 appears on page 187, it should be numbered 187a. (**Note:** ensure that initial caps are used for specific references in the text, e.g., Table 3.1, Figure 4.5, 'Figure 2.7 in Chapter 9', etc., but note lower case for 'the figures in the following chapters'.) Some tables are provided with notes, and these should be keyed in with superscript numbers or letters, not asterisks.

Two figures are reproduced below, with source details set below the figures. (Source details can vary in design detail but are always consistent within the parameters of each volume/book/journal, etc.)

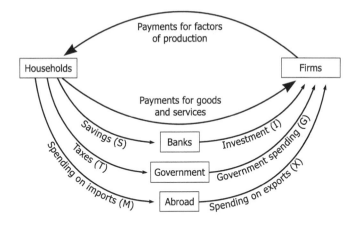

Source: Department of Trade and Industry, *The A-Z of Economics* (HMSO, London, 2005), p. 79.

Figure 2.1: The Circular Flow of Income.

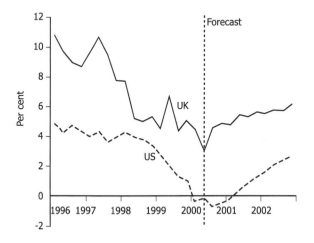

Source: National Institute Economic Review, 4/2000.

Figure 3.1: The Savings Ratio on the US and the UK.

11.2 Tables

Examples of table layouts are given below.

Table 1.1: Number of Visitors to the Haven Leisure Centre (1995–2005)

Visitors	1995	1996	1997	2005
Hotel Guests	28	37	45	50
Members	260	255	285	306
Members' Guests[1]	74	75	84	95
Staff	9	20	21	24
Totals:	**371**	**387**	**435**	**475**

[1] Non-residents.
Source: *Health Statistics Yearbook* (2005).

Table 1.2: *Urban Population in the World and Eight Major Areas, 1925–2025 (millions)*

Major area	1925	1950	1975	2000	2025
World total	405	701	1548	3191	5713
N. America	68	106	181	256	308
Europe	162	215	318	425	510
USSR	30	71	154	245	310
East Asia	58	99	299	638	1044
Latin America	25	67	196	464	819
Africa	12	28	96	312	803
South Asia	45	108	288	825	1873
Oceania	5	8	15	26	38

Source: United Nations (1994).

The printed matter in tables often causes problems for typesetters (whether or not it's digitally printed), e.g. the correct alignment of columns of figures, especially when there are decimal points. They should always be carefully checked.

Note that captions for figures are usually below artwork. Those for tables are above the table. Figure captions usually end with a full point but table captions don't.

CHAPTER 12

The index and second reads

12.1 Indexes

The index is not normally part of everyday proofreading work; this is because the page number references cannot be set until the corrected page proofs have been returned. Indexing is a specialised field and you should have a special penchant and training for it. Books may sometimes need to be 'repaginated' when a hardback is re-run as a (smaller) paperback, so the page number entries will be incorrect. If squash can be described as a specialised form of cardio-vascular masochism, some might describe indexing as a focused form of nit-picking torture, specialising in minutiae.

And yet, people who actually *like* indexing are fairly numerous; they belong to the Society of Indexers, attend conferences, hand out medals to deserving indexers, organise in-house workshops, and charge about £2 a page for their efforts. After indexing his first book, Bernard Levin declared, 'I would rather be dead than do it again.' No less an authority than the *Chicago Manual of Style*, however, states that 'every serious book of non-fiction should have an index if it is to achieve its maximum usefulness'. It's best not to argue with indexers; just leave them to get on with the job. Most of them deserve real praise. (Personally, I tend to agree with the person who said: 'The test of a vocation is the love of the drudgery it involves.')

Indexers now have specialised software to help them, and this must be seen as a boon. Automatically generated indexes/indices lead to some oddities of reference, like floating hyphens, line breaks and misspellings, as well as censure from professional indexers. The software is actually more for helping with sorting, checking autotype, etc. than for generating index entries.

You can find out more about indexing from the Society of Indexers at www.indexers.org.uk.

12.2 Second Reads

A second read is a quick read through the second set of proofs; this is the final check to see whether the corrections marked by the proofreader have actually been inserted correctly. If there was only one error, for example on page 40 (line 5), just check that the correction has been made, and also briefly glance at the surrounding lines to see that they also remain correct.

Reading second proofs can add a little extra income, and they are worth doing. A few hours on a Saturday morning can soon add up to a worthwhile sum, if you can persuade a publisher to pay you the proper rate. Doctors can charge £100 just for providing a death certificate for a patient, probably in less than an hour. To earn £100 doing a second read is going to take you at least six hours, if you're lucky. (An odd comparison, I know. My son's a medical student, and he rang home today, explaining how he'd helped to prepare five death certificates over lunch; he was pleased because if he ever came across five stiffs at lunchtime when qualified, he could earn £500...)

I suppose I'm just jealous. It's hard enough to get into proofreading, *and* make sure you get regular work from publishers. If you believed everything you read, proof-readers would be needed 24/7 by tens of thousands of welcoming editors, falling over themselves to offer you fat cheques for proofreading rubbish written by second- and third-rate authors. It's not like that.

To make any impression at all on those oh-so-cagey in-house editors, you'll need some serious training. In addition, accuracy is not something to be aimed at in proofreading: you need to hit the proverbial bull's-eye with every correction. You need to be good, something special.

Note: from an author's point of view, second reads may develop into third and even fourth reads. There can be query letters with sentences like these: 'There were quite a few widows and orphans which I have tried to eliminate by making and losing lines where necessary . . .'

The proofreader can keep sending you (entirely justified) comments and queries, so the task seems to go on for ever. With the fresh input or deletion of text, new widows and orphans appear as if by magic! The typescript may have been 'post-noted' too, so gaudy coloured slips, or flags, stick out from the sides, alerting you to things that need to be changed later. The prospect of your book becoming finished recedes ever further. It's still great fun.

CHAPTER 13

The proofreading marks or symbols (BS 5261C)

A person starting proofreading for the first time may be anxious about using the correct marks. Some of them may at first also seem somewhat strange. The delete mark, for example, might need a minute's practice or so before you feel confident about reproducing it. It does not have to be an exact copy or replica, just a sign or mark approaching that given as standard. Most of the time you will be using only about half-a-dozen marks, and these are learnt very quickly. It is in fact, in the beginning, more important to be able to notice the actual errors than it is to worry about marking them up correctly. On reflection, they are really quite simple. There is an instruction that you are giving, the 'textual mark', i.e. the mark through, on, over or under a word or words in the text, which **identifies the error** (after you have found it of course!) and the 'marginal mark', which **identifies the nature of the correction.**

Above all remember that you are *communicating* something to another human being – the typesetter/digital printer – so make the instructions 'typesetter-friendly' all the time by being *precise, clear and consistent*.

There were previously two proofreading standards: *British Standard 1219* and *British Standard 5261* (the latter introduced in 1976, and since revised). The two standards were much the same, except that BS 5261 uses marks/symbols only as marginal instructions. With BS 1219, you could write words in the margin, such as 'bold' or 'ital' (for italics) but now you must use marginal marks. The introduction of BS 5261 was an attempt at international standardisation.

BS 1219, an old favourite with many editors, proofreaders, and even typesetters, has since disappeared off the horizon, and has been more or less withdrawn from standard use. To be up to date now, you need to study and use the marks for copy preparation and proof correction from 'BS 5261C:2005', extracted from BS 5261-2:2005. It sounds a bit technical, but the system is easy to understand. You can get a really handy laminated card, showing all the necessary marks, from the British Standards Institution (BSI) for £5.00 (see Appendix III). These are the marks (BS 5261C:2005) that should be used now (2007 onwards), and not those from BS 5261C:1976 (or BS 1219).

New Hart's Rules gives a comprehensive list of marks and is recommended as a reference book. Try also any recent edition of the *Writers' & Artists' Yearbook*.

BS 5261 was originally recommended for dealing with foreign authors and/or printers. In its latest revised form, it has become the one you need to know.

Don't forget to use a **red** pen for correcting the proofs (typesetting errors) and a **blue** pen for marking up editorial errors, overlooked or missed by the copy-editor.

Corrections must be written clearly in the margin, in left to right sequence, adjacent to the line(s) that have to be corrected. Both margins can be used for corrections, the tendency being to write in the left-hand margin for corrections to the left, and in the right-hand margin for corrections to the right, e.g.

=/ the result of police enquiries at Scotlaₐnd Yard. . . 𝄐

What is the difference between a Ⓢolecism and a ≠/
⌐/ non sequitur?

As already mentioned BS 1219 used *words* as marginal instructions (more often than not), rather than mere *marks*, as is now the case with BS 5261. The proofreader would ring round or encircle such marginal instructions, e.g. stet (let it stand), rom (roman), etc.

ⓇⓄⓂ The ⓑⓘⓩⓐⓡⓡⓔ case of the ballet-dancer's billets- Ⓢⓣⓔⓣ
doux. . .

Using BS 5261, this would now be marked up as follows:

4/ The ⓑⓘⓩⓐⓡⓡⓔ case of the ballet-dancer's billets- Ⓥ
doux. . .

If you write an instruction in the margin, which subsequently proves wrong, or you wish to change, you can use Tippex for neater presentation or use pencil to start with and overwrite with pen when you are sure.

If you *do* want to write some comments or instructions in the margin(s) to give further meaning or clarity to your corrections, you can of course do so, but make sure you draw a circle (encircle the matter) around what you've written.

When making textual marks, if you find space is a problem (not enough), or for reasons of clarity, the advice is to circle the affected area instead.

If you have any queries (see **Making a List of Queries** on pages 162–3), use a pencil and write in the margin or use a ringed question mark to indicate the location(s) of the query.

Remember that comprehensibility is more important than absolute, rigid adherence to rules.

Some of the marks that follow may differ in slight respects from the proofreading marks set out in BS 5261C. Everyone's different, and I'm no exception. You try drawing the mark for a change from italics to roman in a hurry, and you'll get some sort of trident looking object that could have been wielded by a miniature Poseidon. If you want to get the best looking marks, and the clearest explanations, do get hold of the laminated card from the BSI, as mentioned on page 102. These people know what they are talking about.

The following are some of the more common proofreading marks based on BS 5261C:2005.

Proofreading Marks

BS 5261C:2005

Instruction	Mark in text	Mark in margin
change to bold	∼∼∼ under words/ characters to be altered	∼∼∼
change to italics	──── underline words/ characters to be altered (or set)	⌐/
change italics to roman	encircle words/ characters to be altered	4/
change to bold italics	under words/ characters to be changed	⌐/ ∼∼∼
change bold to non bold	encircle words/ characters to be changed	∼∫∼
change to non bold and non italics	encircle words/ characters to be changed	4/ ∼∫∼
change to lower case	encircle characters/ words to be changed	≢
change to capital/ upper case	≡ three lines under chars/words to be changed	≡
change to small capitals	═ two lines under chars/words to be changed	═
change small caps to lower case	encircle words/ character(s) to be changed	≠
initial cap(ital)s, rest small caps	≡ three lines, then two lines under chars/words	≡
wrong font - replace with correct one (wrong style/face of type)	encircle character(s) to be changed	Ⓧ
change damaged characters	encircle character(s) to be changed	X
correction is complete/ concluded	none (helps to separate more than one correction on a line)	/
insert in the text the matter in margin	ʎ	new matter, followed by ʎ
insert new copy	ʎ	Ⓐ
delete / or ⊢─┤	strike through character(s), words to be deleted	∂∖
delete and close up	strike through as above, and use 'close-up' mark	∂∖

Instruction	Mark in text	Mark in margin
leave as printed, i.e. ignore printed Latin: 'let it stand'	———— under word(s) character(s) to remain	(previously '*stet*')
invert type (e.g. for inverted comma 'wrong way round')	encircle character to be changed/altered	
close-up - to delete space between chars	linking/bridging between characters ⌒	
substitute or insert character(s) in 'superior' position (e.g. for superscript numbers)	/ through character or where required ʎ	e.g. ʎ or ʎ
ditto for 'inferior' position	/ through character or where required ʎ	e.g.
underline word(s)	——— under word(s) (or circle)	
transpose	between character(s) or words to be transposed	
insert space	/ through character or where required	or #
insert thin space (ball on a stick)	/ through character or where required	
insert space between lines	—(or)—	
reduce space between lines	—→ or ←	
reduce space between words	| between words ↑	
take over character(s) to next line		(extends into margin)
take over character(s) to previous line		(extends into margin)
begin a new paragraph	before first word of new para	
run on text/no new paragraph	between matter	
spell out abbr. or figure	encircle words/figures affected	*spell out*
move matter to right	at left side of matter	
move matter to left	at right side of matter	
substitute or insert full point/stop	/ through character or / where required	⊙

Instruction	Mark in text	Mark in margin
substitute or insert comma	/ through character or / where required	, (or ⌅)
substitute or insert semicolon	/ through character or / where required	;
substitute or insert question mark	/ through character or / where required	?/
substitute or insert colon	/ through character or / where required	⊙
substitute or insert exclamation mark	/ through character or / where required	!/
insert single quote marks	⅄ or ⅄ ⅄	⅋ ⅋ (or ⅋)
insert double quote marks	⅄ or ⅄ ⅄	⅋ ⅋ (or ⅋)
insert hyphen	⅄	⊨⊣
insert en rule	⅄	1N
insert em rule	⅄	1M
insert ellipsis	⅄	⟨ ··· ⟩
insert parentheses	⅄ or ⅄ ⅄	⟨/ ⟩/
insert square brackets	⅄ or ⅄ ⅄	[/]/
insert apostrophe	⅄	⅋
insert oblique stroke/ solidus	⅄	⊘
query anything of doubtful accuracy	encircle words	⊘

Note: These proof correction marks were 'drawn' by computer, to make them neater. There is no need to make exact copies; just use your own style. See page 103 for examples of handwritten marks.

As an example of different styles of marking up, the BSI may say that ‚1N, is how you should mark up for an en rule, but in practice these are still fairly common: ‚N₁, ‚en₁, or just Ⓝ, or N , or ⓔ! The same goes for em rules of course.

Most of the proofreading marks you will ever need to know have been listed above, mainly following BS 5261C. It may seem like learning a completely new language but it's really simple when you come to use the marks; it's certainly nothing like as difficult as trying to get to grips with an actual language (try Farsi, Greek, or Moldavian!). For much of the time you'll use about half a dozen common marks, and if in doubt refer to one of the standard reference books. The *Writers' & Artists' Yearbook* (published annually) has a useful section. [The 2006 edition must have been put together in a hurry, as it contains a fair number of proofing errors!]

A *full* set of marks is available from the BSI. You do have to pay for a *complete* set of marks, but if you study a recent edition of the *Writers' & Artists' Yearbook*, plus pages 105–7 in this book, that is probably all you need to get started.

Appendix III on page 174 gives details of the laminated card available from the British Standards Institution for just £5.00. It shows some proof correction marks not included in the list above, such as how to transpose lines of text, centre text, indent, justify, unjustify, correct vertical or horizontal alignment, and so on. It also includes notes and comments, telling you, for example, that, if you are inserting new copy, i.e. marking up for it, using a reference letter such as 'A' in a diamond shape, then you need to mark the separate piece of paper containing the new copy with the same reference number (to identify it more easily). More copy is referenced 'B',

'C', etc. The card is detailed and precise, and should clarify any queries you might have with the proof correction marks.

Don't think you have to reproduce each mark as a kind of exact, artist's facsimile. Idiosyncrasies in marking up, within reason, are tolerated. If your squiggle can be (broadly) understood, it's probably good enough.

Note that with differences in marking-up styles abounding, there are bound to be differences of opinion. Some people, for example, dislike my use of a 'hat' over a comma. I got used to this because I copied it from someone else, and I think it makes the correction easier to see. The 'experts' say using the 'hat' is *erroneous*. The use of a 'hat' may be erroneous but there was a time when every living typesetter knew exactly what it meant. It's like saying if you write 'stet' in the margin of proofs that it's erroneous. You should just stick with the tick in a circle – so that everyone can understand (by virtue of international standardisation) what is meant. So, to keep the purists happy, avoid using a 'hat' when marking up for a comma, and don't encircle semicolons. Similarly the # sign for a space is little used now but how convenient it was.

The best way to understand how to apply proof correction marks is to start using them!

CHAPTER 14

Practical examples

Let's look at some practical examples:

The idea for the Title of the book came quiet suddenly. If she were to make her *debut*, she had had to ensure that it was going to be somethinng special, a fait accompli from the moment she set fingers to keyboard, It wasnt a particularly brilliant idea, and it wasn't as if she were especially knowledgeable about feline creatures. Except that this was no ordinary cat: she would call the book Wildcat. At 8.30, when the children had gone to school, the house was blissfuly peace-ful. A breeze rusled the leaves of the apple trees in the garden. The Telephone rang. . .

After you have read this carefully, look at the corrections below.

  The idea for the Title of the book came quiet suddenly. If she were to make her *debut* she had had had to ensure that it was going to be somethinng special, a <u>fait</u> <u>accompli</u> from the moment she set fingers to keyboard, It wasnt a particularly brilliant idea, and it wasn't as if she were especially knowledgeable about feline creatures.

└┘ Except that this was no ordinary cat: she would
     call the book <u>Wildcat.</u> At 8.30, when the children ⌐/
ꜱ) had gone to school, the house was blissfull U/
     peace︢ful. A breeze ru︢led the leaves of the apple t/
     trees in the garden. The ⓣelephone rang. . . ≠/

Which will eventually read:

The idea for the title of the book came quite
suddenly. If she had to make her debut, she had
to ensure that it was going to be something
special, a *fait accompli* from the moment she set
fingers to keyboard. It wasn't a particularly
brilliant idea, and it wasn't as if she were
especially knowledgeable about feline creatures.
Except that this was no ordinary cat: she would
call the book *Wildcat*.

At 8.30, when the children had gone to
school, the house was blissfully peaceful. A
breeze rustled the leaves of the apple trees in the
garden. The telephone rang. . .

Note: one mark not mentioned in the previous chapter
above [an excellent example of tautology] is the instruction
to justify. This simply means set the text full out, either to
the left or right margin. 'Range left' or 'range right' is
another instruction you will sometimes see on an edited
manuscript or typescript. At the end of an introductory
chapter, for example, the author often adds his/her name;
this will be marked up as 'range left' or 'range right'
(depending on style), if not typed in the right position. Some
proofreaders have slightly different styles of marking up. As
an example, instead of encircling a letter when marking up
for lower case, the same result can be achieved by:

≠   The Government of the day

or where a heading has been mistakenly set in upper case:

THE BRITISH GOVERNMENT
or
THE BRITISH GOVERNMENT

It does not really matter as long as you achieve consistency and clarity. Note also the marks used to take over (or take back) character(s)/words. You must also be on the lookout for bad word breaks. Look at these examples:

literal-

y speaking

psychol-

ogically

psych-

oanalyse

These now become literal-ly (or take back the -y); psychologically and psycho-analyse. The main rules are a) insert the hyphen where the word breaks naturally into two or more elements and b) insert the hyphen so that each element of the broken word can be pronounced correctly at sight (often the case, for example, with a double consonant). Thus travelling but batt-ling (not bat-tling), miss-ile (not mis-sile), future (not fut-ure), oli-garch (but mon-arch), oper-ation (not ope-ration or opera-tion). Two further points to remember are a) defer to the guiding principle of readability and b) avoid two-letter elements, if possible: on-ly, op-en, etc. Unstressed syllables should never be split, e.g. differ-ed.

You'll soon be ready to move on to the three-part, instant file download from *The Pocket Book of Proofreading* website (**MS1, PS1** and **PS2**). Meanwhile, here's a one-minute **Spelling Test with Proofreading Marks**. Here are two sentences with a total of 15 proofreading marks to be made. 'Spelling' also includes words that should be spelled as one, or hyphenated. The answers are given at the end of the chapter, so try not to look at these until you have attempted the spelling test. The sentences are also repeated again for you to practise making your own marks.

The concensus of opinion was that the innnuendo bore all the hall marks of his priviledged predeccessor.

They sat spell bound, replete with sight seeing and the cries of well wishers, loth to refuse the chance to fullfill their dreams and listen to the peacable ryhthms of the principle band.

The concensus of opinion was that the innnuendo bore all the hall marks of his priviledged predeccessor.

They sat spell bound, replete with sight seeing and the cries of well wishers, loth to refuse the chance to fullfill their dreams and listen to the peacable ryhthms of the principle band.

When you have attempted these, check how you have done. Unlike typescripts, which should be double-spaced, marginal marks in proofs are necessary, as there is so little

room to write corrections. If the corrections seem complicated, don't worry. All the mistakes were deliberate.
Proofreading marks can be learnt very easily, so practise a
few times on a separate piece of paper, and then mark up
the two sentences as above. Mark your corrections with
the typesetter in mind; he or she will be relying on the
clarity of your instructions. Use a red editing pen.

The con∤ensus of opinion was that the innŋuendo
bore all the hall⌐marks of his privileḓged
predec∤essor.

They sat spell⊃bound, replete with sight⊃seeing
and the cries of well⁄wishers, loṯh to refuse the
chance to fulⱡfilⱡ their dreams and listen to the
peacable rħthms of the principḽe band.

Just to remind you, the instructions tell the typesetter (in
order, from left to right) to do the following:

> delete 'c', insert 's'. [The solidus or oblique mark/
>   forward slash (/) means (remember?) that the
>   correction is concluded]
> delete 'n' and close up
> close up (into one word)
> delete 'd' and close up
> delete 'c' and close up
> close up (into one word)
> close up (into one word)
> insert hyphen
> insert 'a'
> delete 'l' and close up
> delete 'l' and close up
> insert 'e'

transpose 'y' and 'h' (hy)
insert 'a'
delete 'e' and close up

Finally, a few other points to consider before beginning Chapter 19 (**Getting Started**). These are prelims; running heads; a note on 'lists'; check-list for copy-editors; and check-list for proofreaders. [If you have sharp eyes, you might find some inconsistencies in Chapters 16 and 18 relating to the word 'check-list'! As a professional proofreader, that's what you'll need to look out for.]

CHAPTER 15

Prelims/running heads/ lists

15.1 Prelims

Prelims (preliminary pages) are the pages that are usually numbered in Roman numerals (i, ii, iii, iv, v, vi, etc.) before Arabic numbering begins on page 1. Here you will find the:

- half-title page (name of book)
- the title page (name of book, name of author, and publisher)
- copyright page with British Library Cataloguing in Publication Data (CIP data), the International Standard Book Number (ISBN number – this is not often set until the last moment; you can mark in pencil 'to follow' in the unlikely event that it might be forgotten, encircled, midway down the page where it will 'go in'). At the foot of the copyright page you will normally also find 'Printed and bound by' or 'Typeset by . . . printed and bound by'
- dedication (or epigraph)
- contents page, followed by
- list of illustrations/figures and list of tables (if

any). In short, the introductory matter to the main text of a book.

The first (right) page is known as the quarter-title page, or quarter-title recto. The copyright page is known as the title page verso. It may also be referred to as the imprint page. **Always make sure that the contents page agrees exactly with the headings/chapter titles in the book.**
You may also have to fill in the page numbers of where each chapter starts on the contents page, and those of the foreword, preface, acknowledgements (if any), list of contributors (if any), etc.

To recap, the usual order for prelims (US: front matter) is as follows: half-title; frontispiece; title-page; imprint/copyright page (bibliographical details, e.g. name/address of publisher or printer in book); dedication (inscription in book to honour relative/friend); contents; list of illustrations; preface (introductory matter to a book, normally written by author); acknowledgements; foreword; and introduction.

Pick up a book now and have a look at the 'prelims'. The format is fairly standard but there are variations. As a proofreader, always check the prelims to check that they are in the correct order for the particular book you are working on, and that there are no glaring omissions.

The copyright © page may contain a copyright notice such as the following:

All rights reserved. No part of this publication may be reproduced, stored in a retreival system, or transmitted, in any form or by any means, electronic, mechanical, photocopying, recording or otherwise, without the prior permission in writing of the Publisher.

Typesetters are so used to setting the above (or a similar version) that you may have to read twenty sets of proofs before finding a single mistake. Did you spot the error? (line 2: retrieval!)

Some publishers really like to go heavy on the legal side of things, and ram home the message with italics, as in this example:

> This book is sold subject to the condition that it shall not, by way of trade *or otherwise*, be lent, re-sold, hired out or otherwise *circulated* without the publisher's prior consent in any form of binding or cover other than that in which it is published and *without a similar condition including this condition being imposed on the subsequent purchaser.*

On the same page the author of the book may also assert the 'moral right to be identified as the author of this work', in accordance with the Copyright, Designs and Patents Act, 1988.

Often there is a fashionable note further down the page that the publisher has used only guilt-free paper(s) – 'natural, recyclable products made from wood grown in sustainable forests'.

The publisher's logo or emblem, by the way, is properly known as the *colophon*. In the case of First English Books, the colophon is two trees, one higher than the other.

15.2 Running Heads

Choose any book at home and look for running heads (a heading at the top of a page). Not all books have them; you'll see that the normal style is: book title – *verso* (left) and chapter title – *recto* (right). [Bless the copy-editor.

She's pencilled this remark in the margin of the typescript: *Not on yours!* (I changed it.) She's also pointed out that sometimes (especially in STM books) an 'A' head will be on one side, chapter title on the other.]

If the proofs have running heads check them as you go along with a quick glance, and note also the pagination (numbers used to identify individual pages; numbering) to see that it runs consecutively and that there are no errors or omissions. Running heads are also known as pageheads.

15.3 A Note on 'Lists'

The great thing about experienced proofreaders is that they know how to define the smallest of the small. I've been proofreading, on and off I admit, for years, and to me 'lists' were just lists. You'll see my attempt at examples of lists below, but I am put squarely and fairly in my place by the proofreader/copy-editor, when she pencils in the margin this succinct observation: 'Lists should be bullets (for no particular order); 1, 2, 3 for order with a) b) c) for sub-orders.'

Here are some examples of lists.

1. 124 baggage animals
2. 14 ten-man tents
3. 13 artillery pieces
4. sundry surveying items

(1) Food for three weeks;
(2) Mining and drilling equipment;
(3) Anti-malaria pills;
(4) Maps and compasses.

a. bobsleigh
b. five pairs of snowshoes
c. satellite monitoring equipment
d. waterproof niqab.

The copy-editor will usually have written 'list' in the left-hand margin, and marked up a line space above and below, the matter to be indented from the left margin.

Look at the spacing and punctuation to see it is consistent, in terms of upper and lower case, semicolons, full points, etc.

Note: I have to add this valuable note (one of many) from the copy-editor after the second read. She's so right. [Please remember, by the way, that the proofreader for *The Pocket Book of Proofreading* also acted as the copy-editor, and, having even more strings to her bow, as the indexer.]

Referring to the 'lists' on page 119, she writes: I still think (!) these should be bullets. [Note the exclamation mark is hers; if mine, it would have been in square brackets.] 1. 2. 3. etc. are for, e.g.:

1. Take out all the pieces and sort.
2. Put legs (A) into top (B).
3. Slide glass (C) into slots in top.

I didn't put her remarks in quote marks as I can see that the first would go in before 'I' but it would look silly putting one in after 'top'; I'll await correction from the copy-editor. I added a colon before the start of the list, plus a full point for etc. It will be the third read before I know if these are right or need deleting. The imaginary 'list' looks so simple; you could in theory try it out on a piece of Ikea furniture on New Year's Day, and not get a stroke fussing around trying to sort it all out! ['If I'd known that my comments were going to be put into print, I might well have written more carefully in the margins, or generally lost the will to live.' *Copy-editor*]

CHAPTER 16

Checklist for copy-editors

Since you will have become familiar with the house style, a straightforward copy-edit chosen for you to work on is often the best way to begin. The **Checklist for Copy-editors** is not exhaustive and is given so that you know what the copy-editor has to do; familiarity with the whole concept will make for better proofreading.

The copy-editor will have to:

- establish agreed points of style
- impose a consistent style throughout
- check headings, subheadings and sub-subheadings
- correct spelling, ensuring consistency
- check grammar/syntax
- see that the paragraphing and layout are the most suitable
- check references in the text against lists of references and vice versa
- see that references are in alphabetical order (or correct numbered order
- mark up figures and tables as necessary
- make a note of any special indents or material that may need special 'design treatment'

- match chapter titles exactly as they appear in contents list in prelims
- number text folios consecutively if necessary
- note any unusual characters/symbols/diacritical markings (mark multiplication signs – not capital 'X')
- see that captions for figures and/or tables are consistent with text
- make a separate list of any queries
- consider if any material could be construed as potentially libellous, and note
- identify superscripts and subscripts (if any) (e.g. ^{6}, $_6$) – mark in margin, e.g. Jones^7
- code headings in descending order of weight/importance, if author has not already done so
- re-type/print out any handwritten material if more than four or five lines long, especially if none too legible (don't expect help from amanuenses)
- italicise uncommon words, phrases, etc.

The copy-editor must mark all corrections legibly and completely, and may be asked to use an erasable coloured pencil, using coloured slips for queries.

Proper names, dates, places and events should be verified wherever possible – query if in doubt – or contact the managing editor.

There's no doubt that a skilled copy-editor needs a nose for good English and it helps to be a knowledgeable tactician. The author's style must not be altered, or gratuitously meddled with, yet the copy-editor ought to be able to distinguish between good and sloppy writing usage, as in (taking just one example) the fine distinction between *infer* and *imply*.

Query also ambiguities, anachronisms, contradictions, non sequiturs, oxymorons, parochialisms, repetitions, solecisms, tautologies, etc., and submit a **style sheet,** noting all proper names, places, unusual spellings and compounds (see below). Sexism: use of he/she or s/he should be avoided where possible; ensure that 'they' always refers back to a plural. Rewrite the sentence if possible.

Here's a very quick guide to some of these words:

- *non sequitur* – a statement that has little or no relevance to a preceding one; it does not follow. '*The Beagle* set sail in 1831. My left toe is aching.'
- *oxymoron* – contradictory terms/words together, such as *cheerful pessimist* or *honest lawyer.* (The proofreader writes in the margin, opposite '*honest lawyer*', 'Will you get sued?' Proofreaders obviously do not need legal knowledge, for example the likelihood of a written remark amounting to libel, but they should be aware how useful it is to draw attention to questionable material. I know the age of deference is no more, ever since I saw David Dimbleby on *Question Time* ask the Lord Chancellor what he thought about something or other. 'So Charlie,' he said, casually turning to Lord Falconer of Thoroton, QC, 'what's your view on this?' My view is, 'Yes, lawyers will sue you, if they can get half the chance.')
- *parochialism* – words that have more meaning for the writer/author than the reader: *He met her last year, not far from here, near Westminster Bridge.* Where is 'not far from here'? Which year is meant? Parochialisms are not changed in dialogue, naturally.

- *solecism* – bad grammar, innit?
- *tautology* – saying more or less the same thing, as has already been said.

When you're on the lookout for ambiguities, contradictions, tautologies, etc., expect some [mainly pleasant] surprises when you need to check word meanings or spellings. It's what makes copy-editing and proofreading such fun. My scruffy 24-year-old dictionary in a sun-faded jacket, for example, gave me a surprising second definition for 'tautology': a proposition in logic that is always true, as in *either the sun is out or the sun is not out*. Just a note of caution: there's never time to discover all the secondary considerations – when for example the sun is only half, or a quarter out, or partially hidden by cloud, so as to be neither out nor in. . . The publisher just wants the typescript or the proofs back, to use that despicable phrase, 'done and dusted', so you'd better hurry up!

CHAPTER 17

Style sheet

Here is an example of a style sheet (or design memo). It's like an editorial prescription listing essential style points, letting the proofreader know what to expect. It may be provided by the in-house editor via the author, or by an industrious copy-editor. Not all publishers use them but as an aide-memoire, style sheets are very useful, and helpful when you're a little rusty yourself.

Authors and translators are not expected to copy-edit their own work. *New ODWE* describes a style sheet as an 'editor's list of forms preferred in a text'. As such, no style sheet can resolve all possible problems. It should simply be regarded as providing guidelines on the difficulties that can be encountered when those involved with the typescript fail to observe any usual conventions; style sheets may also prevent a large number of errors from having to be corrected at proof stage.

Instructions to follow a particular reference book may be given, and for spellings, there might be a note, such as: 'Please use all preferred spellings in the *Oxford English Dictionary*.' Copy-editors and proofreaders should always get in touch with the publisher's in-house editor(s) to discuss points of style if there are special features not covered in a style sheet, such as large numbers of tables or extensive transliteration from foreign languages.

Please return to
Title *The Politics of Modernism* ⟨ XY *publisher*
subtitle *Against the New Conformists*
author/editor *Raymond Williams*

contents *YES* ✓   preface *(Editorial Note)*
acknowledgements *YES* ✓   introduction *YES* ✓
epigraph *NO*   bibliography *YES* ✓
dedication *NO*   index   *YES* ✓
list of tables *NO*   running heads *YES* ✓
notes: foot of page/⟨end of chapter⟩/end of book
~~-ize spelling~~/-ise spelling   ⟨A⟩/B/C/D headings
English/~~American~~ spelling
English/~~American~~ punctuation
special sorts *spell out numbers under twelve*
special layouts: tables/lists/interviews/verse/. . .
spaced EM dashes in text ✓
unspaced EN dashes between figures (1939$\frac{1}{N}$45)
single quotes, double within single
mark all end-of-line hyphens for retention or for close-up
   and delete

ABCD	EFGHI	JKLM
avant-garde	*Fascism (historical*	*Left (noun)*
(roman; hyphen	*noun movement)*	*left (adj.)*
+ adj.)	*fascism (general)*	
Cultural Studies	*Formalism (h.m.)*	*Liberal Studies*
	formalism	

NOPQ	RSTU	VWXYZ
post-structuralism	*utopian (lc)*	*wellhead*
outraging	*Right (n.)*	*(one word)*
	right (adj.)	*Zollverein (itals)*
	Structuralism	
	unmistakable	

Note: proofreaders get good and bad days, just like anyone else. Sometimes, you just can't draw a straight line; you mean to insert a caret (⟨) between two letters in a word and succeed only in 'deleting' one of them. In the same vein, you'll see the 'Z' in *Zollverein* in the list above is just about the strangest looking capital 'Z' going. It's either got a neck like a giraffe or it's an impressionist swan. Who ever heard of a *Zollverein* anyway? Who cares? That's the point. As the proofreader, you don't get any say at all. You just read the words!

House style notes or style sheets may be more detailed than the example above, some amounting to ten or more pages. They can be quite useful. Here are a few quick samples:

- Titles should be capitalised (initial letter in capital) when they precede the name, but not otherwise: Minister of Climate Change Bickerstaff. . . *but* Bickerstaff, the minister of climate change. . .
- Compass points are capitalised only when they designate a region: in the North of the country *but* Ralph Fiennes trekked north. . .
- Historical eras are capitalised: Dark Ages, the Mesolithic
- In general, capitals are discouraged; use lower case when in doubt
- Spell out numbers less than 100; so ninety-two *not* 92. Exception: when there is a series of numbers where at least one number is greater than ninety-nine, other numbers should be in figures too: In 2007 there were 195 dentists in the region; after the revolution only 26 remained. Compare this with other house styles, e.g.: spell out numbers one to nineteen; figures for 20 onwards

- Avoid hyphens in compounds already hyphenated: a 32-year-old priest *not* a thirty-two-year-old priest *but note:* he was thirty-two years old *not* 32 years old
- Do not use a hyphen for foreign phrases used as adjectives: laissez faire ideas; a posteriori principle
- Hyphenate object plus present participle: eye-catching colour
- Punctuation that is part of a quoted phrase should remain inside the quotation marks
- Superscript numbers in text indicating notes should always follow punctuation: in these sources.[2] *not* in these sources[2]. Note an exception where a note indicator refers to material within parentheses, in which case it is placed inside the parentheses: in these sources[2]) . . .

And so it goes on! Having a recommended reference book on your desk when proofreading (especially one that's up to date) clearly helps.

The Society for Editors and Proofreaders (SfEP) publishes a useful online style guide in its 'Editing Matters' section. You can read it by checking out this PDF link (www.sfep.org.uk/pub/mag/mag_sg.pdf), for which you'll need Adobe Reader.

CHAPTER 18

Checklist for proofreaders

Fortunately, the copy-editor will have done more than 95 per cent of the points in Chapter 16. Your job is just to see that the typesetter has set everything as instructed; so you'll be looking for 'typos' or print errors, or 'literals' – misspellings when the copy-editor 'nodded'. [At this point, the copy-editor adds a hyphen to that word (copy-editor), it having been previously missed by both of us. She cheers me up by writing 'nod . . . nod . . .' in the margin. One thing leads to another; I know it has something to do with Homer, but what? Before looking at the answer below, ask yourself truthfully, do you know the source? I find the answer in a dictionary of quotations: Horace (might as well do the Ben Schott thing – *Quintus Horatius Flaccus, 65–8 BC, Roman poet whose* Odes *and* Epistles *portray Roman life in great detail*). In *Ars Poetica*, he wrote: 'I'm aggrieved when sometimes even excellent Homer nods.' I'm happy to have found this out. It's annoying to know half a thing but not all. If I'd been copy-editing or proofreading this page, I'd have made no money for the past 15 minutes. There were another 46 Horace quotations to read, and just about every one is entirely memorable.]

Since you'll have the typescript alongside the proofs, you can see what the copy-editor has done, so as you read you'll become aware (or should do!) of any minor inconsistencies that have been allowed to pass by the copy-editor. Remember how useful it is to pencil in a mark in the margin so that you can refer back quickly to anything of which you are uncertain. When you have resolved a particular point, erase the pencil mark. Use post-its for quick referral to your own queries. Remember also to make sure the house editor has sent you a style guide (see Chapter 17). As you become more experienced you will need only to refresh your memory at the outset.

The proofreader will have to:

- ensure a consistent style has been used throughout
- check for any errors in spelling, layout, headings, etc.
- check all running heads, page numbers, cross-references, prelims, etc.
- check to see that page depths are not too short or too long, in other words be ready to spot an obvious case, say a page three lines short for no reason
- fill in page numbers on the contents page; check the number corresponds to the correct page in the text
- mark up typesetter's errors in red, editorial (copy-editor's) in blue unless proofreading on-screen
- make only such changes as are absolutely necessary, i.e. keep them to a minimum
- make a separate list of any queries you may have, including if you are unsure as to whether to change something

- make or suggest improvements or changes as necessary
- draw attention to any apparent/unresolved queries by making a query in pencil in the margin
- use the correct (BSI) marks; use them neatly and correctly (BS 5261C:2005, and *not* BS 5261C:1976 or BS 1219)
- be sure, if there is more than one correction in a line of text, to mark up the proofs in left to right (marginal) sequence, separating or ending each correction with an oblique (solidus)
- treat, if marking up (or deleting) accents/ diacritical marks, the character plus mark as one entity. Cross out the entire [Here the proof-reader adds a caret mark, with an encircled question mark in the margin. The entire *what* is the question. It's terrible; it's a long afternoon. The first word I can think of is *caboodle*, the *entire caboodle* – that's character plus accent. So now it would read: 'Cross out the entire caboodle...' It sounds marginally better. I'm not sure if I can get away with 'entire' here as a noun, when often it means an uncastrated horse. A daydream begins. I'm with Fitzgerald's *Rubáiyát of Omar Khayyám,* trying 'to grasp this sorry Scheme of Things entire', so it could be shattered to bits, then remoulded nearer to the heart's desire! Will there be many more queries, I ask myself?] in the text, writing the correction in appropriate margin, followed by an oblique
- be aware of inconsistencies, ambiguities, repetitions, etc., as well as any potentially libellous material, missed by the copy-editor.

(Don't imagine that the copy-editor is infallible. He could well have been distracted by Scarlett Johansson, she by Brad Pitt or Toby Stephens. You can never be absolutely certain. It helps to develop a questioning mind.)

- **read** conscientiously, carefully, and **collect the rewards!**

Note: a proofreader's work is never done. Just as you think you've mastered all the pernickety rules and conventions of good proofreading, everything can suddenly change. You might realise it when leafing through a reference book, or looking over how the copy-editor has tackled a subject. 'God,' you'll exclaim sotto voce, 'I didn't know that!' For example:

- Book and film titles are always italicised but books of the Bible (and house names, poem and song titles, etc.) are usually in roman.
- Avoid gender bias (even if fatally attracted to Eva Longoria).
- Beware mixing up singular and plural when verbs are around. Here's a macabre example from a newspaper. Would something like this catch you out? Perhaps not, but it might depend on whether you lose concentration after reading such a preposterous yet true story. 'A ring of gangsters who traded in the bodies of women they murdered, selling them as brides to keep dead bachelors happy in the afterlife, have been arrested in China.' (Singular 'has' is needed, to agree with 'ring'.)
- Use different *from* and not different *to*; use compare *with* and not *to* (except when comparing

favourably, as in 'Shall I compare thee to a summer's day?' (This perfect example, from Shakespeare's sonnet 18, is the proofreader's.)

- Allow 'dissimilar to'.
- You can say the choirmaster 'is forever chasing choir boys' but the dean 'wishes everyone the love of Jesus, now and for ever', which is quite different, as 'for ever', as two words refers to a very long time indeed – eternity – not something happening regularly, i.e. continuously.
- Do you know about buying stationery on a stationary Virgin train?
- Are you familiar with (correct usage of) comparatives and superlatives? For instance, comparatives like *better, elder, greater, higher* or *less*, etc. compare one with another (that's two items/things/persons) but superlatives like *best, eldest, greatest, highest* or *least*, etc. compare themselves with two or more other items/things/persons. So Rupert is the elder (of two) but Irena is the eldest of the three.
- It's the same with *between* and *among*: share Christmas presents among several people but between two.
- The simple word *none* catches many people out; the word means 'not one', so an accompanying verb has to be in the singular too. 'None has seen Eva and Archie share a kiss' is correct, not 'none have'. (Talking of bears, here's a quick reminder of the difference between a *homonym* and a *homophone* (cf. antonym/synonym). A homonym is a word of the same form but with a different sense or meaning; a homophone is a word spelt differently but with the same pronunciation. The

words 'bear' and 'bare' on the front cover are homophones. I had intended to give a third example: 'bare as in Eva Longoria – naked?' but my 13-year-old son was horrified, and so this example (which in any event the proofreader had pointed out as 'last two meanings are the same') was deleted. I then wasted more time, telling myself that it was quite true that the 'bare' in 'bare, ruin'd choirs' was just the same 'bare' as in Eva Longoria – naked. However, wasn't there a delicate difference between, say, a row of leafless elm trees in winter and a disrobed Eva? One 'choir' is empty; the other is overflowing with abundance, yet both are '*bare*'. The conclusion? 'Sweating the small stuff' is not always such a great idea!)

- As for the wars concerning 'on to' and 'onto', let me explain. It seems that *on to* is generally always acceptable but sometimes (and it may depend on publisher and house style) you may need *onto*. In the US, *onto* is standard. In the UK, you can use *onto* (accepted as a word in its own right); however, if it's possible to infer some sense of position between one and another, especially (so I have read) one *atop* the other, as in 'Archie climbed onto Eva', that's all right. However, 'Archie started coming on to Eva' (two words). Where 'on' is considered to be part of the verb, use two words: 'He moved on to the next platform.' Compare with 'He jumped onto the next platform.'

There are so many other things to look out for: World War II or the Second World War (style, thankfully); is it

Halloween or Hallowe'en; would Archie and Eva be equally as happy in each other's or one another's arms? 'Equally as' is a mean tautology; so just say 'equally happy', and as for each other and one another, I plead a cop-out. *I don't know!* I'll have to look it up . . . Fowler explains it. (By the way, it's 'cop-out' with a hyphen (noun) but 'cop out' (two words) when a verb.)

Generally, if you're reading against copy, you can lean on the copy-editor. The copy-editor can be your best teacher for polishing all those rusty memories of grammar oddities like mixed metaphors, the correct use of *you and I/me*, *who/whom*, *less* and *fewer*. Of this last or last-named (remember to use 'the latter' when only *two* items are in question), Fowler gives a neat example. '*Less tonnage*, but *fewer ships*' (i.e. is it countable?). Trust the copy-editor, and your luck. Editors aren't going to give the job to just some dumb schmuck, are they?

Let's hope you can depend on the copy-editor, most of the time. Follow the rules of consistency and common sense. Apply them judiciously. Using common sense wisely means that you can also break the rules. If there is no house style guidance, for example, and numbers are used *consistently* in centuries, you can leave them (8th century, 18th century). You don't need to change them to the more commonly used eighth century, eighteenth century (i.e. follow the usual convention, which is to spell out centuries). Although this is more a question for copy-editors than proofreaders, it still pays to know.

If you need to find out more, I did warn you it's only a pocketbook . . . I'll have to stop somewhere too, or I'll never finish the book.

* * *

This part of *The Pocket Book of Proofreading* is now complete. The next chapter is on **Getting Started.** Did you see the inconsistency? In para. 4, line 2 on page 135 above there is 'pocketbook' but in line 1 above: *Pocket Book!* Admittedly, the latter is part of a title, so you could excuse the difference. You really need to go back to 'pocketbook', and ask yourself, if you were the proofreader, should it be 'pocket book'?

In my sun-bleached dictionary, there is 'pocketbook – *chiefly U.S.*, a small bag or case for money, papers, etc.' In my equally old and well out of date (1981 vintage) favourite reference book, the since superseded *The Oxford Dictionary for Writers and Editors*, I'm reading 'pocket-book (hyphen)'. Help! I'm beginning to understand why the proofreader is right to advise getting rid of old reference books. It's taken me months to appreciate this simple fact. I'm going to check in the most recent edition I can find (2005), and see what the *New Oxford Dictionary for Writers and Editors* has to say.

[Naturally, it doesn't change my opinion about Archie. Thank God (or post-Dawkins, god) no one ever attempted to throw him out for being old-fashioned, and not up-to-date enough.]

In the book shop, an assistant checked, and the screen read: 'received'. I collected something that quite bowled me over; it was fat and sexy at the same time, small and smoochy, with a distinctive pebbly dust jacket, the kind that makes you want to keep looking into a pool of clear blue water filled with attractively shaped stones. The *New Oxford Dictionary for Writers and Editors* (subtitled 'The essential A–Z guide to the written word') is so beautiful, and on the back there's an an endorsement from the Society for Editors and Proofreaders (SfEP – www.sfep.org.uk), who are in turn complimented in the Preface by *New ODWE*.

I went straight to 'pocketbook' (one word), along with 'pocketknife'; 'pocket money' and 'pocket watch' were two words; and 'pocketful *pl.* pocketfuls', was thrown in for good measure. 'Pocket handkerchief' (two words) has been quietly dropped from the new edition, and 'pocket battleship' was sunk a long time ago – it never featured either in *ODWE* or *New ODWE*.

Just out of interest, I had to check 'book shop' (see above). All I got was: 'bookplate, bookrest, bookmark' (all one word), interrupted by 'bookshelf *pl.* bookshelves', then 'bookstall, bookwork, bookworm'. So book shop it is, although it's surely 'bookstore' in the US. [This is superbly 'confirmed' by para. 1, line 3, p. 146! And on page 147.]

The book is certainly a big improvement on earlier editions. I'm happy to see eye to eye with the proofreader now. *New ODWE* is so desirable to an editor – you'd want to keep it under your pillow! It's the *ne plus ultra* of editorial reference books.

[Sorry Archie, I'm losing faith in you ever so slowly. You really do look scruffy, lop-eared and tired. Your body parts seem assembled from different sources. You could do with some serious sprucing up.]

One minor point worth a very quick mention is to do with the (correct) alignment of numbers, for example, chapter head numbers on the contents page. It's a fairly common error. You may see, for example,

8.
9.
10.

when what you should see is:

8.
9.
10.

Try to enjoy your work, like it's exciting and not some kind of menial chore. It's true sometimes that the work can be very tedious, for example checking columns of figures, such as the billions spent by the government on the NHS over the past twenty years. You're not being paid just for 'reading' but for the exercise of very definite skills that can take a long time to acquire successfully. On the bright side, suddenly you can be asked to proofread the equivalent of David Attenborough's *Planet Earth*, and it's leaping off the page at you, and you're there, exploring some magical corner of the earth. Wow! You'll think, is someone paying me to do this? Well, yes, they are but only as long as you do the job properly. So reality checks from time to time are always a sound idea.

Note: in Appendix IV, you'll find some short exercises. Use these to practise your proofreading skills! (And by the way, on page 137, did you notice any inconsistencies in para. 2, line 6? There's 'p. 146' and 'page 147'. You have to discover the golden mean of good proofreading: consistency.)

CHAPTER 19

....

Getting started

If you like the idea of becoming a freelance proofreader or copy-editor, and have followed the various sections so far carefully, more say than catching up on the news by watching *Have I got News For You*, then you will already have learnt and assimilated a great deal.

Now you can continue if you like by logging on to *The Pocket Book of Proofreading*'s website where you can download the three-part proofreading course, consisting of **MS1**, the typescript of *Santorini – A Greek Island*; **PS1**, the uncorrected proofs of the story; and **PS2**, the corrected proofs – all in an easy-to-download PDF file.

Look closely at **MS1** because it's an example of copy-editing and should help you gain greater understanding of the subject. You can read it in your spare time. Try to absorb as much as you can. You'll find clear instructions on the website if needed. In just a little while, you can be working your way through the proofs, and gaining the knowledge that you need for success.

MS1 is not meant to be a literary masterpiece but a practical step to teaching you how copy-editing works (easier than consulting a textbook). It will also help you to understand how proofreading works too. In my book, understanding a little about copy-editing is a big step to understanding proofreading.

Please don't consider the editorial style as *the* way to edit. You may even find a few places where you could improve the style – if you were the copy-editor. Use **MS1** for your own ideas, and note how the typescript/ manuscript is marked up. It's not exhaustive but it will serve as a real beginning. When you come to make your corrections on **PS1**, the uncorrected proofs, remember that red is the right colour for correcting typesetting errors, and blue for editorial errors.

You can download **PS1**, the proofs of the story, and **PS2** (the corrected proofs) all in the one file. Don't forget the *Extra Exercises*, two extracts from a new novel (*Hold Your Head Up High*), for even more proofreading practice.

Computers and the Internet are changing the way publishers work. A lot of proofreading and editing work is still managed in the usual way – that is, typescripts are sent by post for proofreaders or copy-editors to correct and return. You'll find plenty of experience is needed, however, before you can contemplate proofreading on-screen. If you can master the skills involved, you can perhaps look forward to using your PC to edit/correct files for publishers on disk.

Personally, I much prefer working with 'paper'. There *seems* to be more scope for deliberation and reflection when turning over the pages of an author's typescript. No doubt another generation will beg to differ! Authors are all different too. Some are error-control freaks, some are just messy illiterates – you'll wonder how they ever manage to get published.

Some top-selling authors still write everything out in scratchy longhand in 50p (lined) notebooks you can buy from W.H. Smith or Spar. Other writers cling to their laptops. They can't write a word unless they've powered up their 'baby' with more gigabytes than you'd need for a moon landing or a media event with Madonna. In fact, they'd sooner decapitate 'Sir' Archibald Ormsby-Gore than surrender autonomy over their precious laptops.

Note: when you choose to download the proofreading course is entirely up to you. Do try the practice exercises in the back of *The Pocket Book of Proofreading* first (Appendix IV, pp. 176–82). It's advisable to familiarise yourself with the subject a little more before starting on the Santorini proofs. The exercises will give you some basic training in using the proof correction marks.

All in all, there's no hurry, so if I were you I'd enjoy the ride for the time being, and travel hopefully.

CHAPTER 20

Finding work

Traditionally, proofreaders were not supposed to 'enjoy' their reading material too much in case enthusiasm for the subject meant reading too fast and glossing over errors. A more realistic view is that, if you enjoy your work (and the subject), then your powers of concentration and ability to sustain interest will quite naturally ensure that your work is up to standard. There's more detail in later chapters about finding work in proofreading; consider this as just the preamble.

Some years ago, I decided to pack a 500-page copy-edit in my suitcase when I booked a short holiday to the Greek island of Santorini. To be a freelance editor appealed as a novel way to pay for the trip. In the stifling heat and only a one-minute walk away from a taverna, which sold some memorable retsina, I didn't find the task of reading through 500 pages an easy one, but I persevered.

A month or so after I got back, a cheque arrived in the post! To have been able to sit in the sun, in the shade of a welcome taverna, and be paid well for a few hours (hours'?) work a day, seemed like the essence of being a freelance.

Intrigued by the word 'freelance', I looked it up in a dictionary. I knew it meant a self-employed person, especially a writer or artist, one who is not employed continuously but hired for specific assignments.

Looking further into an American dictionary, *Webster's Ninth New Collegiate Dictionary*, I found three wonderful definitions of the noun *freelance*, first used in about 1820:

> **a:** a knight or roving soldier available for hire by a state or commander
> **b:** one who acts independently without regard to party lines or deference to authority
> **c:** one who pursues a profession without long-term commitments to any one employer.

It's still possible today! The Internet continues and extends this remarkable tradition for those who are able to take advantage of it.

When you start work, the first priority is to be aware of the kind of errors that you are looking for; once you have learnt, for example, about the pitfalls of capitalisation, are aware of points of style, and know your punctuation, you are already beginning to equip yourself with the particular kind of knowledge which, once practised and mastered, will come naturally to you – just like any other skill that has to be acquired, learnt and mastered before it can be put to good use. **Practising** those skills is the quickest route to success.

If you decide you are going to make a success of it, plan ahead. You will need self-confidence and determination: make a positive, definite decision that you *are* going to succeed. There is no harm, after all, in believing in your own abilities.

Just make sure you bring a professional discernment to bear on the project in hand; if you try and give your best, you will never be disappointed. Your self-confidence is a precious asset. Build on it a piece at a time.

There is no need to rush blindly forward. Spend a few days going over what you have already learnt. Practise the proofreading marks. Pick up some books and mentally glance over the design, layout and style of each one. Visit any local bookshop and/or library. Grab a Starbucks, and settle back with something worth reading. You can quietly remind yourself that of the hundreds, if not thousands, of titles on view, nearly all of them will have been 'read' by freelances, all of whom will have 'made money from reading', and made a career out of it as well. Don't forget these are the lucky ones, though. To succeed, you need some pretty serious skills, and be tough enough to get your toe in the front door!

When you have succeeded in getting your first set of proofs, always pay careful attention to the work of the copy-editor. In effect, just by reading through the typescript, which will accompany the proofs, and taking note of the marked-up copy, you will be getting *FREE LESSONS* on how to copy-edit. The advantages of becoming a copy-editor are that the rate of pay is better, and there is more opportunity to exercise your editing skills – all of which leads to more satisfaction at work. Copy-editing offers more freedom of choice and is more creative. A major benefit is that you can often double the amount of work you are able to do.

If you are asked to copy-edit a book, you may well be asked to read the proofs as well, effectively doubling the fee. However, beware proofreading your own work; it's much better to let someone else discover your weaknesses! To be able to copy-edit and proofread is also a way of making sure that you are kept busy all the time. However, there are some proofreaders who would prefer not to copy-edit and vice versa. The two are such closely related skills that to master both is usually far better. Don't consider that one is better than the other, that copy-editing is somehow superior – even though a copy-editor earns more. A good proofreader is worth his or her weight in gold.

Never underestimate the value of training, whether you want to work as a proofreader or copy-editor. People need training for both jobs. Contact SfEP, the Society for Editors and Proofreaders or the Publishing Training Centre (web addresses and more information in Appendix III, pp. 174–5).

Overnight success, be warned, is extremely rare. Your first set of proofs is *the* most important one: from then on you will have had experience, however limited. Keep on good terms with the in-house editors and strive always to offer a truly professional service; if you are keen and willing, the chances are that they will return to you with more work. After a while they may even become close friends, able to rely on you to get work done quickly and effectively. The amazing thing is that even professionals need training and a bit of investment in what they are doing or they get out of form. CPD (continuing professional development) seems like the best solution – all the way along!

Of course it's not just books that need to be copy-edited and proofread. A stream of marketing material falls out of magazines (in addition to the success of books like Harry Potter and other bestsellers), all tribute to the enduring power of the printed word.

Note: you'll find literally masses of other material where you can demonstrate your skills and earn good money: websites, brochures, reports, catalogues, company leaflets, dissertations, and so forth.

CHAPTER 21

First priorities: plan of action, contacting publishers

A sensible first step is to obtain a copy of the *Writers' & Artists' Yearbook* (*W&AYB*), which you can find in any local reference library, bookshop or online (price around £13.99). Apart from containing a lot of information connected with the publishing industry, it also has a useful section on proofreading marks, and contains *a list of hundreds of UK book publishers* giving essential information, as well as book publishers in Australia, Canada, New Zealand, South Africa and the USA.

The *W&AYB* gives the following:

1. alphabetical list of publishing houses
2. full address and telephone/fax numbers
3. names of directors and managing editors
4. subjects published

Let's look at item 4 in more detail. Some typical entries are:

> *Biography, children's books (fiction, non-fiction), cinema, sports, crafts, travel, humour, leisure, literature, health and beauty*

> *General non-fiction, history, biography, travel, gardening, food and wine, health and beauty, art, design, photography, antiques and collecting, music, politics and contemporary affairs*

> *Business studies, computer studies, accountancy, finance, politics and economics*

From such a diverse list you should be able to choose half-a-dozen publishers to begin with who work in subjects or areas that may be suitable for you.

Perhaps you already have several hobbies or interests where knowledge in certain subjects would be an advantage.

Experienced proofreaders, however, almost always **do not need specialised knowledge for general subjects.** What matters is whether you know the essential rules – the groundwork for which you have already learnt.

Find out from sources of information, such as the *W&AYB*, Yellow Pages, local library or bookshops whether there are any publishers near you. Some publishers prefer working with 'local' freelances. The *Writer's Handbook* is invaluable, not least because it has an exhaustive subject index.

Distance, however, is not of overriding importance. What matters is *whether you can do the work*. Virtually all publishers in cities employ freelances to do some editing, most copy-editing and the majority of all proofreading. The only advantage in living near a publishing firm is that you can call in to meet your editors when you have been given freelance commissions; you can also deliver the proofs back in person, and so get known by the people you're working with. Some firms, whose editorial staff is quite small, rely on freelances in both editorial and art responsibilities, have freelances all over the globe, and are always interested in developing new help for their projects.

The main objective at this stage is to get your name known to publishers. You'll need to compose a letter on good quality, standard size (A4) paper explaining your interest in obtaining freelance work. Send in your 1-page CV with your letter if you have a particularly good one. Don't write lengthy paragraphs but be precise and businesslike. Experiment with different formats to see which gets the better response. (Apparently, the 1-page CV counts for a lot, and I have this on good authority, passing on this tip as I do from the assiduous proofreader.) You can enclose an sae if you wish. Also try faxing some of your letters, and some publishers prefer emails with an attached CV!

If you're lucky, you'll receive replies in due course and may be told that your name has been added to their files. Thus your first step has been accomplished. This does *not* mean that you will necessarily receive any offers of work at all, but you now have a contact name, and you can follow up your first letter with another and/or phone or email.

In fact, the best tip I learnt from an experienced freelance editor is **always** to follow up your initial enquiry with a call soon afterwards, or a fax or email, while you're still 'hot' in the in-tray.

Publishers and in-house editors usually have a 'pool' of freelances from which to draw as and when necessary. If someone has a holiday or there is more work available, just by being 'on file' could bring you an offer of work. This is why a properly thought out and well composed letter – in the first place – is something to take a great deal of care over. Make sure there are no spelling errors and don't offer subjects to publishers who don't publish in them.

A typed or printed letter is absolutely essential. If you have headed paper so much the better. When you subsequently find success as a freelance, you should have letterheads printed (your name, address, together with phone number and email address). Describe yourself simply as 'Freelance Proofreader/Copy-editor'. You can hyphenate (proof-reader/copy-editor) if you like but the modern trend appears to be as one word. Purists prefer 'copy-editor' in the UK. (You can design and order stationery online, e.g. www.surfprint.co.uk. Compliment slips are useful too, especially when you can mention membership of the SfEP.)

Your emails can also carry a 'signature line', such as your name and particular skills (e.g. proofreading and/or copy-editing), and the kind of books you specialise in, if any (e.g. history, cookery, medicine, etc.).

Note: some mail-order companies selling proofreading courses provide a 'standard' letter for you to copy, but if you send off a standard letter, you'll probably just get a standard response! You need to be different, stand out, individualistic without being over the top. It's no use saying something like, 'I've loved reading books since I was a child', or something indescribably naff such as, 'I'm *so* interested in books; it's like I was born to be with them!'

If sending a letter, make sure your address is correct. Cut out unnecessary punctuation. Don't put commas or full stops in the wrong places. Make sure the place names or roads are correctly capitalised. If you sent out a letter with an address like this, you probably wouldn't even get a reply.

24 Whitesheet Lane
Wigan
Lancashire
WN24 2PD.

What's wrong? There should be no full point after the postcode (or in dates)! Common mistakes also include 'Thankyou' instead of 'Thank you' (two words), and 'Yours Sincerely' instead of 'Yours sincerely'. Even with emails, you need to take special care. Treat dates with respect too (best to stick with this format: 1 September 2007).

This is one letter from someone in America looking for copy-editing work. This might work fine in the States, but not in Britain. No editor is especially interested to know that you love to correct 'grammatically-challenged sentences'. (Strictly speaking, a hyphen isn't required, see page 54.) Notice how the letter ends 'Sincerely'. That's correct for the US. You need to use either 'Yours faithfully' or 'Yours sincerely' for letters in the UK (the first on beginning a correspondence with someone new; the second for a more established relationship), but this rule doesn't hold on the Internet.

Hello,

I'm a copyeditor in search of freelance work. I love to correct grammatically-challenged sentences, and I'm very good at rewriting for clarity and simplicity.

For 12 years, I've been proofreading and correcting other people's work. I did have my own business as a scopist for 5 years. A scopist is someone who fixes transcription errors, proofreads, and edits (not verbatim quotes) court documentation for court reporters. All case documentation exchange was done through the Internet.

In the last 5 years, I was a technical writer for Hewlett Packard. I wrote many technical documents, but I would also proofread and edit engineering technical documents for non-technical and technical audiences. I've worked on hundreds of documents over the course of my time at Hewlett Packard, and I've rewritten several server manuals for their server division. I've worked with both online documentation and hard copy.

Please let me know what your procedure is to find copyeditors for the books that your company publishes.

Thank you!

Sincerely,
Cloey H.

Make your letter or email short, professional, and to the point. Ending with the typically effusive American usage, 'Thank you!' is not recommended in Britain.

Lots of people ask the chicken and egg question. How can I get work if I haven't got the experience, and how can I get experience if I haven't worked? My advice is: *blag it!* Lots of people have done just that. Don't give away too much. Just be businesslike and to the point.

Blagging it doesn't mean telling lies – more like being economical with the truth. Don't own up to a complete lack of experience. Set out your letter properly.

But why not get some training first? The SfEP offers a fairly cheap introduction to proofreading (and copy-editing), and workshops to see if you are suitable or even like it. It saves a lot of heartache later. They also run annual conferences, cosy affairs where you are actually made to feel you belong. There's always something new on the agenda because dedicated proofreading and editing sleuths are hard at work the rest of the year tracking down the finer points of interest. Their newsletters contain articles tailor-made for freelances.

You can make this your first objective: getting your name on file with a number of suitable publishers. Don't be disheartened if you seem to be making slow progress; very few people make a success of their own business from the first day. Most of the time they are preparing and thinking ahead, gradually getting 'in front' a little more each day. If you are keen, determined to succeed and have some ability, you *will* succeed. All the preliminary work you have had to do will all seem worth while.

Just a few years ago 'worthwhile' was one word when used *attributively* (before the noun modified) and two words when used *predicatively*. I still don't completely understand the entire grammatical explanation of 'predicatively', except that it's to do with something happening *after* the noun. It's correct to write 'a worthwhile sum' (page 99, para. 5) but note how you can use 'seem worth while' (two words), as in the paragraph above. However, the latest edition of *New ODWE* plumps for either one *or* two words predicatively, after the noun, making 'seem worthwhile' now acceptable – yet another example of the proofreader being right and Archie facing the chop. I mean the old reference books should just be admired in big glass cases.

With hyphens, compare: 'Tony Blair awaits news from the cash-for-honours investigation' with 'The investigation is all about cash for honours' (see also **7.12 Hyphens**). If you're thinking of using your common sense, it's always two words, but add a hyphen when used attributively, as in 'a common-sense reaction'. I suppose it's only the ace copy-editor who knows that 'common sense' is always two words predicatively but worthwhile can be *either* one word or two!

How long this will last is anyone's guess. Horace, he of *Carpe diem* fame (see also page 129) has a word to say on this, as one of the earliest copy-editors: 'Many terms which have now dropped out of favour, will be revived, and those that are at present respectable will drop out, if usage so choose, with whom resides the decision and the judgement and the code of speech.'

Your happiest moment could be the first day a publisher contacts you, and asks if you are free to work on a set of proofs. It is never wise, to coin a familiar saying, 'to give up the day job'. Remember that anyone who succeeds in business or any kind of creative venture has usually had to work for it, and to get your first success in publishing will likewise require effort and determination.

Aim to build up gradually. Just think: if you could be working for four or five publishers within six months, or even three or four, what sort of reward could you expect? If you become known as reliable and efficient, editors will be only too happy to place work with you. To find a good proofreader or copy-editor means that they can keep to *their* schedules and, if you can communicate well on a personal level, they will enjoy working with you and vice versa.

A book a month from each publisher is about average, sometimes two books a month. Most successful freelances have between five and six books at any one time on their desks waiting to be proofread or copy-edited. Payment varies from publisher to publisher and depends on complexity and length. A 350-page book may take about 35 hours, so at £17.50 per hour, you would collect a cheque for £612.50, copy-editing slightly more. Four books a month of this length means an income of £2,000 or more a month, a pleasurable way to earn money if you need it.

If it takes several months to find your first one or two publishers who will regularly send you work, remember that you need to find only another two clients and your earnings potential will double. It's only when you have established your contacts that you can choose to work either full or part time; in the beginning there is little choice; it is most unlikely that you would be working full time.

Remember that if you only have one client, you cannot claim freelance status, and the taxman will be after you! You must have at least three clients in order to be classed or classified as 'freelance' for tax purposes. Check with your local Tax Office. [Don't you just love those homely suggestions? Just ring your local Tax Office. Not 'tax office', either. Who says it has to be Tax Office? The proofreader, of course! 'Erm, hello? Should I be paying tax on this gargantuan cheque?' We must all toe the appropriate line but I remember some good advice, nothing to do with tax, obviously. Never volunteer any unnecessary information.]

Once you have work coming in, however, this is when **_and only when_** you can decide whether to seek more work or just accept one or two books a month if you prefer to work on a casual, part-time basis. [A number of people have used _The Pocket Book of Proofreading,_ plus the online proofreading course, to find in-house work with various publishing companies, e.g. as editorial assistants. They may have started out wanting to find freelance work, but by chance they were offered work as editorial assistants, proofreading in-house and learning all about the publishing business. It's an irony of current life in publishing that most publishers accept only graduates and most of them can't spell!]

CHAPTER 22

Tests

Some publishers will send you five- or six-page tests before deciding to put out work to you. These may look deceptively easy and simple but **be warned!** You must take extra care as they have been designed to really test your skills. [Split infinitives become more acceptable every year.]

Many of these tests are the work of editors doubling as fiends. They are so clever they could complete *The Times* crossword before you crawl to the end of the first paragraph.

You don't need to find every single error or inconsistency but you must demonstrate real, natural ability rather than just being average or below average. Beware simple errors of grammar, where editors will try to catch you out. Here are two simple examples:

> If I was a rich man, I would . . . (*wrong*)
> If I were a rich man, I would . . . (*correct*)
> There are a plethora of other small fish that are also
>   fried. (*wrong*)
> There is a plethora of other small fish that are also
>   fried. (*correct*)

How many letters or emails should you send so as to place your name on file and with luck obtain work? It depends naturally on the amount of effort you want to put into it. To begin with you should aim at making **one or two good contacts;** 'use' them to gain more experience.

22.1 Certificates

Some mail-order firms offer 'certificates' for completing courses. That's fine, if you like hanging something on a wall. Publishers, however, take no notice of them. They mean nothing, other than that you have completed a course. They confer no academic honours and are just used to increase sales of their mail-order courses. The same applies to some fancily named 'Diplomas'. Beware those courses that promise the earth, or try to trick you into believing it's simple to earn vast amounts of money almost overnight. You'd be far better off with the SfEP. Most decent publishers accept their accreditation methods. So, if you're looking for something worth having, an investment that actually means something, check out the SfEP website.

[A company selling 'proofreading courses' flogged many other courses, including one that promised to get you 'a flat stomach in seven days'! Mail-order companies love to try all the tricks. A favourite one is to tell you that whatever they are selling actually costs double the price, but if you buy it now, you can have it for only half-price! Imagine you're just going to buy a new Mercedes from a car showroom. It's listed at £60,000. The slick sales guy tells you it's really worth £120,000 but, if you get your cash out now, you can save tens of thousands of pounds.]

Publishers are interested only in whether you can pass a short test, which they may or may not send you (see above), and whether you have bothered to get any training, such as from the SfEP or the Publishing Training Centre. If you pass one of these tests, you may then be placed on a list of freelances, and whereas it's still no *guarantee* of work, it's a good beginning.

Having recommended the SfEP incidentally, do bear in mind that people who run these kinds of organisations can sometimes behave towards others like little tin gods. Although I have nothing but praise for the SfEP, it may be true to say that some of the longer-serving 'officials' are just a little bit too proud of themselves as arbiters of style/taste/usage. They clearly spend too much time on minutiae, and need to get out more.

Personally, I would occasionally be chary of their gigantic 'expertise', and in some respects would not recommend them with open arms, other than a nod in their general direction. Like self-appointed guardians of morality, a few of these guardians of the proofreading world rarely see much further than (just) in front of their noses. Getting them to say a good word about anybody can be surprisingly difficult – unless you are fortunate enough to be the author of a '*standard* reference work'. I'd simply refer them to Horace (page 153).

It's possible I'm writing this in 'self-defence' in case one of the SfEP reviewers mauls my little book in any review. They're going to get me, I'm sure, for allowing 'hats' on commas, and for encircling semicolons. Well, I'll just have to accept the criticism. After all, they're right, and despite the unkind words from me about 'little tin gods', they're probably still 'the best in the business'.

On page 145, incidentally, you'll find 'Harry Potter'. If it's a book title, why isn't it in italics? Is 'Harry Potter' a proper title? Learn to be a proficient proofreader by challenging any such anomalies and you might just pass one of those fiendish tests!

CHAPTER 23

How to generate more business

A useful publication in the UK is *The Bookseller*, read by over 15,000 publishers every week. Their address is: The Bookseller, 5th Floor, Endeavour House, 189 Shaftesbury Avenue, London WC2H 8TJ (www.thebookseller.com). The classified section has a FREELANCE WANTED column, which sometimes contains advertisements from publishers looking for freelance proofreaders and copy-editors. Once you have gained a reasonable amount of experience, you could consider advertising your services in the FREELANCE OFFERED section. Most public libraries keep copies of *The Bookseller*, which you can refer to. Advertising rates are very reasonable.

Some trade journals have classified sections where you can advertise your services for a small fee, and once you have gained more experience, you could consider this method.

Keep an eye on your local press, as there are sometimes opportunities for proofreaders other than working for publishers.

For the adventurous or ambitious, International Book Fairs, usually held annually at a prestigious venue, offer unrivalled opportunities to meet publishers, editors and just about anyone who has an interest in the world of books. Freelance editors and proofreaders can enter on 'trade only' days when the public is not admitted. You'll find mostly sales personnel, and few editorial staff, but they do try and pass your card on.

For a small fee you will be issued with an identity badge with the word FREELANCE in capitals, and there are stands taken by all the major and smaller publishing firms with books and catalogues on display.

On a good day you'll find editors – the ones you might be working with as a proofreader or copy-editor – there on business to take orders, and answer questions. A business card is always appreciated. For those with the desire to learn more, Book Fairs are an excellent meeting place. The London International Book Fair, usually held each year in March or April, is very popular

Some successful freelances travel each year to the Frankfurt Book Fair. A day's 'work' can result in commissions lasting several months. In fact, a friend of mine visits each year and stays with friends, either in Frankfurt or Cologne. Some years ago, when I asked him how successful his last trip had been, he said: 'Funny you should ask that – I've just been adding up the totals so far from the Book Fair, and I'd say it's brought in an extra £10,000 in the last six months!' You should consider Book Fairs as a new source of work, however, only when you have gained a reasonable amount of experience.

If you are fortunate enough to know someone in publishing (perhaps a friend), this could be a contact leading to work. Do not fret if you haven't. Concentrate on writing crisp and clear businesslike letters to introduce yourself to publishers asking if they have any work for freelances.

CHAPTER 24

Rates of pay and invoicing

24.1 Rates of Pay

At present the hourly rate of pay for freelance proofreaders depends on finding a generous publisher! Fortunately, there isn't yet a surfeit of 'overseas proofreaders' willing to undercut the meanest rates. The recommended or suggested rate (from the SfEP) from April 2006 was £17.50 per hour. Some firms have adopted a new system where you are asked for an estimate of your fee when the proofs arrive. A few publishers themselves fix a flat fee for a particular job, but this seems, essentially, to defeat the purpose of going freelance.

A fair number of publishers will offer you less than the going rate, especially if you are a beginner. It usually pays to accept their offer because the essential first step is to find work, your first set of proofs.

If you were reading fiction (e.g. a Western) you would probably be expected to read 14–15 pages per hour (the number of printed lines on each page is considerably less than for a standard non-fiction book) – otherwise, about 10 pages per hour. Time yourself in the beginning. If you make an estimate that falls short of the actual number of hours worked, you are generally allowed to add on the extra time taken. Copy-editors also work on about 10 pages an hour. Sometimes the typescript may be near perfect and an experienced copy-editor might prepare 15 pages an hour. If the same level of care is taken, you can still charge for work done at the standard rate.

24.2 Invoices

Invoices should be printed out or typed with your name, address and date, etc. (as in a letter), and the name and address of the publisher, followed by (example):

To proofreading (TITLE OF BOOK in capitals)
by (author's name)

hours (number of hours) @ £ (agreed rate) per hour £
plus p&p/padded envelope/courier service   £

TOTAL   £

Proofs are normally returned by first-class post unless otherwise instructed, e.g. special delivery/courier service.

You should find sending the proofs back quite satisfying – as long as it hasn't been one of those particularly awkward jobs you'd prefer not to remember. Your invoice has been sent back along with the proofs, and maybe it's been a typescript that's been stimulating to work on.

There's the occasional flash of humour. I remember one job where the in-house editor rang to ask me oh-so-discreetly if I would 'mind' proofreading the lascivious memoirs of a certain Mayfair 'Casanova'. Mind? Not when the rent has to be paid. It was a Monday morning when I began, my partner had already left for work, and outside rain gently fell on tea roses blossoming in the garden. Within five minutes I was straight into the story – rustling petticoats torn off on the first page as the rutting rake attempted to work his wicked will between her willing thighs. . . There are of course more sobering occasions, such as when proofreading a harrowing account of victims of Nazi war criminals.

Some proofreaders can be picky. A female proofreader working on the proofs of 88-year-old Doris Lessing's latest book, *The Cleft*, refused to continue working on them because she thought the language too explicit. Shame!

Allow at least one month before receiving cheques for work done. Some publishers may pay sooner than this but the average is between four to six weeks. The benefit is that quite a reasonable sum can sometimes accumulate before you receive payment. If payment is late, you can always contact the publisher concerned, and the query should be dealt with straightaway.

Cheques are paid without deduction of tax or national insurance (i.e. gross). Do bear in mind what tax inspectors consider 'freelance' to be (you need a minimum of three clients in most cases). Keep a record of work done and cheques received. You will be expected to make your own arrangements (self-assessment) with regard to income tax. A good accountant can often point out items that can be claimed for. Don't worry about this aspect yet: just keep a careful record of expenses and payments received.

24.3 Making a List of Queries

If after reading your proofs there are any unresolved queries, print (or type) out a list of them on a separate piece of paper. If the in-house editor cannot resolve them, the query list will be forwarded to the author. Even at proof stage, queries have a surprising habit of surfacing but they will probably be quite minor.

A useful query if you were proofreading *The Pocket Book of Proofreading* would be to point out that some 'turnover' lines in displayed material or quotes are not indented. Compare 'He caught the trout. . .' on page 48, second line not indented, with 'If you go down to the woods today. . .' on page 55, where the turnover line is indented. Consistency is the rule, so one of your queries should be: 'Are turnover lines in displayed material all to be indented, as there are [give examples] inconsistencies?'

Note: you should not use a query list to find answers to questions you are unsure about. Don't expect an in-house editor to explain the difference, for example, between infer and imply. A quick answer, if you don't know is 'speakers imply, listeners infer'. You'd be looking at an error if you saw in the Review section of the *Observer*, 'The title definitely infers . . .' (This handy example *is* from the *Observer*, 22 April 2007.)

Editors always appreciate proofreaders who take the trouble to query anything they are uncertain or 'unhappy' about. Sometimes there will be nothing to query, where the proofs are 'clean', the text straightforward.

Nearly all copy-editors will have started as proof-readers; after gaining suitable experience, the in-house editor may ask if you'd like to try a copy-edit – or you can always ask! (Rates for copy-editing vary between £16 and £22 per hour and normally for this – as a rough rule of thumb – you would edit about ten pages per hour.)

Note for copy-editor: an inconsistent use of hyphen occurs in the first line of the paragraph above. To be consistent, it should be 'proofreaders'.

CHAPTER 25

Benefits of the Internet

The Internet is incredibly exciting and useful, and it saves money. If you are dealing with an author (or an editor) in Korea, for example, and want to send a ten-page fax of queries, it can cost £10. The same message via email costs under 10p, and it can cost nothing! The Internet shows an exponential growth rate worldwide.

Recently I emailed a friend who has worked as a proofreader and copy-editor for many years. How busy was he? Back came the answer: rushed off his feet. A few days before an author had sent him a 400-page typescript for correction. With broadband, it had taken him just a few seconds to download all 400 pages!

Some freelances spend £300–£400 a year on couriers (getting the work back quickly to publishers, which would be reimbursed) but at least the publisher can send by email a few files instead of physically posting lots of paper.

Many publishers are now looking for people who can copy-edit and proofread 'electronically', using a PC with appropriate software. The files are simply sent by email or on a CD by post. Proofreaders would need Adobe Acrobat Reader to read the proofs, but if you are to proofread electronically, you would need the professional version and guidance from the publisher as to what needs to be done.

Some training companies and publishers run one-day courses just to enable proofreaders to make the transition from paper-based to on-screen mark up. If you can make use of these new skills, you can expect to be busy. The Internet has empowered individuals, and it's likely to become even more integrated into our lives in the future.

The Internet is *the* place for opportunities and new contacts. Google, the world's biggest Internet search engine, has nearly 90 million unique users each month. By the time you read this, it will surely be 100 million.

Note: there are hundreds of websites offering free resources for writers and editors. Here's one, a free online dictionary from Cambridge University Press: www.dictionary.cambridge.org.

Sony is developing a new gadget, the Sony Reader (Sony Portable Reader PRS-500), an iPod-style device that allows readers to download and store about 80 books. Each virtual page turns more or less at reading speed, and it will 'do' 7,500 page turns on a single charge. Sony's eBook has a 6in screen and supports a range of formats including PDF, TXT, RTF and Microsoft Word files, so you can read your own content instead of buying it. Text size can be adjusted too. The device won't put proofreaders out of business. Proofreaders and copy-editors will be needed for thousands of new books.

Learn to develop your skills and you'll find many new doors are there already, just waiting to be opened. Proofreading really is fun!

CHAPTER 26

Postscript

You now possess the knowledge to go ahead. Remember all the skills you have already learnt, and think ahead positively. There is always competition, as is only to be expected, but you can *prepare and help yourself* with a patient, methodical and professional approach. The market for freelance work is thriving and healthy. I hope the following scenario may soon be yours.

From: ajones@xy.publishing.co.uk
Date: Wed, 27 July 2007 18:29:03
To: john@edits.merlin.co.uk

John - I have received your fax asking about freelance work for XY PUBLISHING. Sorry unable to reply sooner due to annual holiday

If you are still on this number and this email reaches you, could you please call me on 0171 000 0000 asap

yours

andrew jones - managing editor

XY Publishing Co. London
29 July 2007

Dear John

How to Run Your Own Travel Business

Thanks for your call. I have pleasure in enclosing the page proofs and MS for proofreading as agreed.

Please mark typesetter's errors in red and any editorial corrections in blue. Errors should have been corrected at copy-editing stage but **please do look out for any misspellings** – especially proper names (e.g. I've just noticed Collossus [Colossus] of Rhodes, p. 104).

I need the corrected proofs back by 3 September. Please could you also phone or email me asap, to give me an estimate of your fee.

I'm glad to hear you have lots of work!

Best wishes

Andrew

Managing Editor

PS: I have a job coming up next month that involves some on-screen editing. Let me know if you can help.

APPENDIX I

......

Publisher's letter

Here's an example of the kind of letter you might receive when you have completed *The Pocket Book of Proofreading* course, or some recognised form of training, and have started looking for work. This one is from a publisher in London.

Dear Stephanie,

We're currently in the process of recruiting freelance proofreaders and, as your details are on our file, wondered whether you would be interested in this type of work. We do have proofreaders we use quite often so would not necessarily be able to guarantee regular amounts of work but we are currently finding that we do have not have enough freelancers to cope with demand.

The way we normally work is to give you a ring on the day that we receive proofs of a book, tell you the extent, subject, date for return, and then negotiate a price if you were interested. We normally work on a fixed price per job (to include return by recorded delivery), rather than by an hourly rate. Some jobs are put out by hourly rate and our rates are currently £17.50 per hour.

We would normally allow 2–3 weeks for any job, again depending on the urgency and length of the proofs involved, and would expect you to check the proofs against the original manuscript and correct any typographical errors and inconsistencies in style or spelling.

If you would be interested in working with us and would like further details, I would be pleased to hear from you, indicating your preferred subject areas.

Yours sincerely,

JEANETTE SMITH
Assistant Editor

Download details and testimonials

Appendix II has two 'parts'. The first part tells you more about the PDF download from *The Pocket Book of Proofreading* website. The second part lists just a few of the many testimonials received.

Follow the instructions on the website and soon you'll be working on the proofs of *Santorini – A Greek Island*. If you haven't already done so, you should find the exercise a bundle of fun!

One of the more flattering remarks received about the three-part proofreading course was that it was much more interesting than crosswords. I've no idea if the same applies to Su Doku. What I can say is that there's just no telling what kind of work might come your way. It depends on what publishers you are lucky enough to work for, of course, but imagine the choice: a few hours struggling with Su Doku or would you prefer to read the proofs of, say, *The God Delusion* by Richard Dawkins; a short discourse on *Muslim Veils and Christian Crosses* by the Archbishop of Canterbury; or the autobiography of Eva Longoria, the glittering Beyoncé; or even *My Life With Archie*? Far-fetched, I know, but *some* people get lucky! (It's more likely you'd get: *The Mating Patterns of*

Pond Sticklebacks; *Celebrity Makeovers in Mid-Wales*; or *Eating Quality Californian Walnuts Can Save Your Arteries.*)

MS1 shows you how to copy-edit a typescript. Then you'll work on **PS1**, the uncorrected proofs of the story. You'll probably go through a range of emotions while working on the proofs. At times, it will feel madly frustrating, then change to supremely enjoyable. If you've visited any Greek island on holiday, the subject should 'come alive' as you read through the proofs.

I'll bet you will be surprised later to discover how you could have missed mistakes that, in retrospect, will seem so obvious. This includes the less obvious errors, too, ones you probably wouldn't have spotted unless you'd gone thought the proofs about twenty times!

Just read **MS1** first, and take note of the contents. Then move on to **PS1** (the uncorrected proofs) when you're ready. This is your test so, before starting on it, re-read the section on proofreading marks. Equip yourself with red and blue editing pens, a pencil, an eraser, and a dictionary. Say to yourself that you are going to find 99.9 per cent of the errors. Practise in pencil first or make another copy of **PS1** so that you can have more than one attempt.

Whatever you do, do not look at **PS2** (the corrected proofs) – YET – as it contains all the answers. Read through **PS1** at least twice and see if you can find anything that you missed the first time.

Finally, check your answers off against the corrections given in **PS2**. A self-assessment scorecard is to be found at the end of **PS2**. Simply count all your corrections and measure them against the score levels given. (Do remember that in a set of 'clean' proofs you may have to read ten pages or so before finding a single error.) Most of the errors in **PS1** are deliberate so you can test your own skills. (**Note:** as a copy-editor or proofreader, never allow yourself to be lightly lulled into that false sense of refuge or security, believing all's just about perfect – the typescript or proofs so squeaky clean that you need take less care. Nothing in writing can ever be taken for granted. Dr Johnson said, 'Shakespeare never had six lines together without a fault. Perhaps you may find seven, but this does not refute my general assertion.' So take care not to miss anything, even when all seems faultless.)

Watch out for editorial errors missed by the copy-editor; mark these in blue on **PS1**. Mark up all the 'typos' in red. When you have checked off your answers, and measured your score level with the scorecard, mark up any additional/uncorrected errors on **PS1**.

From the website (www.pocketbookofproofeading.co.uk) you can download **MS1** (the typescript), **PS1** (the set of proofs for you to correct) and **PS2** (the corrected proofs). Don't forget to get the free *Extra Exercises*.

Note: help is always available 24/7 by email for any questions you may have. You can also arrange for the full course to be posted to you if you prefer. Please see the website for more details.

When the download is complete (a few seconds with broadband), print out the complete course when you're ready, using your own printer, on good quality A4 paper. You'll need approximately 130 to 150 sheets of A4.

You'll also find a list of 'uncorrected errors' and other points of interest. How well you do could determine whether you'd make a competent proofreader or not. Don't be too disappointed if your score is not that perfect. Practice is necessary for nearly everybody. You should enjoy working on the story about the Greek island. It's great fun. I'm sure you will enjoy every word!

Good luck and good reading.

Some testimonials received about the proofreading course

I've been told by the copy-editor (who is also the proofreader) to limit the number of testimonials, although there are many. She says they sound too self-congratulatory, just 'puffs'; and it's 'slightly off-putting if there are too many puffs'. I'm not going to argue with her now, so here are just a few:

Thought I'd let you know where your course has now led me! I have recently begun work full time for an Internet news group as a sub-editor. Little did I know that, when I did your course 18 months ago, it would result in me securing full time employment from home with my first ever invoice for £1,000 about to be issued. I have the champagne on ice . . .

I have now completed the course and must congratulate you on this masterpiece. I have read a lot of 'guides' recently but none more informative or friendly. The information on how to get started is invaluable.

I wouldn't hesitate to recommend The Pocket Book of Proofreading, *and the unique online three-part course, to anyone who yearns to work for themselves or just find out more about the work of a proofreader or copy-editor. My thanks and regards.*

I've had four jobs so far with (xxx) Publishing, and am really enjoying the proofreading assignments from them. I still have four tests out, and plan to do some more marketing . . .

Thanks very much for sending your course material, which I received before Christmas. I am now starting work and would be pleased to receive the update you mentioned in your email. PS: You may be interested to know that your course was recommended to me by a friend who is an established freelance copy-editor for a leading University Press.

I have to say that your book, online course and website were a great find. It is great getting paid to read. When I tell people what I do, they can't believe it. Sometimes I can't either.

Just a quick email to say thanks again for all your help. I've had a bit of luck and the first publisher I called offered me work! I'm now working on my second book for them, with promises of more to come.

It was a course that changed my life and has given me a career that I love and the flexibility to stay home with my son. Getting paid to read is like heaven on earth! I have three regular clients that give me all the work I want to pick up right now. Taking your course gave me the courage to take the plunge and go for it.

Have just finished my <u>sixth</u> book for them (a well known London publisher).

I'm loving every minute of it – I am so happy that I decided to enter the 'scary' world of proofreading and copy-editing! Thanks again! Best wishes.

APPENDIX III

Useful addresses

Get an incredibly useful laminated card showing the main copy preparation and proof correction marks (BS 5261C:2005) from the **BSI**. Simply send a cheque for £5.00 (add £4.00 postage) to: BSI cash office, P.O. Box 16206, Chiswick, London W4 4ZL. Make your cheque payable to 'British Standards Institution'.

The **Society for Editors and Proofreaders** (SfEP) is 'a professional organization based in the UK for editors and proofreaders'. It aims to promote high editorial standards and achieve recognition of the professional status of members and associate members. It is worth joining for all the latest news and info, plus training and accreditation. Find out more at www.sfep.org.uk.

The **Society of Indexers** exists 'to promote indexing, the quality of indexes and the profession of indexing'. The SI is a respected institution, and they tell you on their website that by 'joining the Society of Indexers you will become part of a group of fellow professionals who are working towards raising awareness of indexes and the profession of indexing. Experienced members are generous with their support and encouragement for new entrants and you will find our networking opportunities invaluable.' You can find out more at www.indexers.org.uk where there are details of membership, training and workshops.

The **Publishing Training Centre** is 'committed to giving you sound advice (without giving you the hard sell)', and is a leading, 'recognised training provider for book and journal publishers'. To find out more, visit www.train4publishing.co.uk.

APPENDIX IV

Sample exercises

Exercise 1

These sample exercises can give you some basic training, and you'll be curious to see how well you do. Marking up in pencil is the best way to start. Write the total number of errors you find at the bottom of each exercise; then add all together (exercises 1–6) to find your final total score. (Don't try to improve the English in Exercise 1, even though you might be tempted! Just mark up any typos and literals; 'light' copy-editing allowed.)

CURICULUM VITEA
Never mind the perfect cv, how about this one

To: The Managing Director
Im just the graduate your looking for! Im keen and motivated and have definately got ideas of how to make things go, so I think Id fit in fine with whatever your company does. Ive got great people skill's and a GSOH and have a fantastic cv which im sending so that you can get back to me. At the end of the day you'll want someone who can think out of the box so if your firms got openings going let me know. Heres my cv, Im sure you'll like it!

Education: Past all my exams that I took, including GCSE, and got a top degree in Nuneaton social college where I did youth and sports studies.

Work experience: Great range of top plaicements including helping assistant manager in local nightclub bar and work with government office in plaicing asylum seekers and checking on them. Have worked with custermers in some big stores and gained meaningful experience in inter-personal relations and business and am qualified in top management issues and out of the box thinking, also work with Windows98.

Travel: Have travelled widely and been to football clubs all over Europe and also Spanish coasts or "costas" and seen some really exotic places in Thailand. Picked up enough Spanish and other languages for good interpersonal relations and have 24/7 attension-span. I'm great with new ideas, and have a cool attitude if things get hot, especially in a business situation. Also like football and grayhounds and other top sports. Played drums in school band so would be good for your social ocasions

From an editorial in *The Times*, 4 August 2006.

Exercise 2

Visit Well's, England's most smallest city and enjoy the wonderful cathedral with its famous scissor arch, magnificent west Front, atmospheric charterhouse and knights who joust each quarter–hour on the 14th century clock.

Explore the mooted Bishop's Palace. Pesvner described it as 'the most memorable in all England.'

Walk in Vicars Close, one of the oldest streets in Europe.

It is lived in now by vicars choral, Cathedral staff, and by boarders from near-by Wells Cathedral school.

Follow the stream of water from the Wells flowing from the nineteenth-Century conduit down the High street to another Church, St. Cuthbert's church itself often mistaken for the Cathedral.

If you walk alongside the curving moat you may see boy and girl's from the Cathedral school which has been in existence for almost 1,000 years. The schools' motto is Esto Quod Es, and is latin for 'Be yourself,' or 'Be what you are.'

From a tourist guide to Wells, Somerset.

Exercise 3

I regard it as one of the best pleasures in Life to have a large glistening fish, straight out of the depths of the sea and on to the charcoal in a prefect island setting. My favorite fish for this purpose is the 'second category' fish, *melanouria* (saddled beam), a flat, fleshy, dark silvery fish with a black line down the lentgh of its body, and *skatharia* (black bream, very similar but even flatter than the melanouri, with a hint of golden rays on it.

Rena Salaman, *Greek Food* (Fontana, London, 1983), p. 213

Exercise 4

It lies very low on the water, with only the small hill of *Cynthus* to hold it from floating away. The blue and violet seas wash its shores, and the winds are fresh and sweet. In Spring it is a mass of flowers, whole sheets of anemmones flooding the meadows filled with gleaming columnsand ruins glittering like bones. In summer it is parched, with thistles and barleys growing thick among the ruins, and in winter the winds of the Agean pour over it, smoothing out the folds of the draperies of the few remaining statutes.

One should come to Delos on one one of those transparant-blue mornings when the sea is very still and the meltemi is blowing softly. One should come leisureley in one of the black boats belonging to the Naxian fisherman, whose skins have turned to leather.

Robert Payne, *The Splendour of Greece* (Pan Books, London, 1964), p. 70.

Exercise 5

Zippy was a little wild. You could see it in her eyes, the wildness of the heathland even the mysterious wetlands, yet they could also be soft softer than violet.

One night she bought Rick the Gypsy to the bar. He was a young buck with a firm, toned body. The DJ. Was playing a record: *Are you ready, are you ready for love. Yes I am, yes I am.*"

Rick heard the words, then jumped up ready to dance. He pulled girls to the dance-floor, and anyone else too. He drank pints. Sweat streamed down him. Rick pulled off his shirt. He danced in the middle of the bar, crazily, exstatically, occasionally shaodow-boxing an imaginary punch bag. The sweat still ran on his broad back and deep chest, healthy and taned by the hottest summer for at least one hundred years.

A crowd gathered, including the landlord, and shaven-heade bouncers, expecting trouble, but Rick kept on smiling, dancing, laughing, joking, taunting - a taut wire string of testosterrone energy. He danced like he had a dragon scorching his feet too, but he just did'nt care. He was to *alive* to do anything else.

The author, *Hold Your Head Up High* (First English Books, Poole, 2005), p. 386-7.

Exercise 6

One of your visits to Santorini must be to the coast where good-tempered fishermen can be seen sitting on the black volcanic sand drying or mending their nets. There is happyness simply in being near the sea, in watching the waves in the sunshine, in breathing the fresh air, in the taste of salt on your lips. Kamari and Perissa are not only beautifull beaches, but picturesque fishing villages as well.

DURING the day fishing boats land there catch of fresh fish, the fishermen bronzed and weather-beaten, acustomed to hard-ship and peril. The increase in tourism over the past ten year has meant that fishermen have ben able to to keep their nets, and more and more tavernas rely on local fishermen to bring in their harvests from the sea.

Sandy Beaches

A new road now joins Phira to the sea. The best beaches, as men-tioned above, are those of Perissa and Kammari. There you will find restaurants, tavernas and hotels from simple *pension size to four-star luxury.* In these seaside places the foothills of Mesa Vouno come down to the beach, and you can smell the scent of thyme and wild flowers from the hinterland.

You can feel the breeze coming of the open blue sea and fill you lungs deeply with sweet-smelling air. You can swim in the crystal-clear sea, then stretch out on the the black sand under the hot sun, or have a rest under the shade of Tamarisk trees. When it is time for lunch you can go to a nearby restaurant and be tempted by its succulent, freshly-caught fish.

At Kamari there are several new and modern hotels which provide luxurious accomodation but you may be equally happy renting an inexpensive room near the sea-side, where the facilities are basic, but comfortable.

Perissa beach is also a wonderful place in the south of the island. It is a fine stretch of coastline—it's famous black sand made up of tinny particles of sand and stone. perissa is blue sea, black sand, and blue skies; a formula that attracts thousands of visiters every year.

However some will lament the arrival of an airport large enough to handle big jets from all over the continent. There are restaurants and beachside tavernas where, after your swim, you can simply be lulled into a state of phsyical and mental relaxation: the warm blue sea only yards away: a plate of black olivio, tomatos and fetta cheese, sprinkled with oil and herbs; a glass of cool white santorini Wine at your elbows.

Centuries ago a small Church was apparently buried beneath the site of the present five-domed church at Perissa. In 1835, a villager had a dream that he should digging begin on the site, and so it was that the old church was brought to light. In a well nearby was found an Icon of the Panahgia and a bronze Cross. Some villagers beleive even to-day that illness can be cured just by drinking water from the wells. Just behind the well is a roman monument while near the feet of the mountain can be found the ruins of an old church (Santa Irini).

From *Santorini – A Greek Island* (First English Books, 2007).

(You can download the full text and free exercises from the website: www.pocketbookofproofreading.co.uk.)

Note for copy-editor: do mountains have 'feet' and if so, how many? See three lines up, last paragraph of Exercise 6 above.

Corrected exercises

Proofs with Corrections and Notes

Exercise 1

CURICULUM VITEA

Never mind the perfect cv, how about this one

To: The Managing Director

Im just the graduate your looking for! Im keen and motivated and have definately got ideas of how to make things go, so I think Id fit in fine with whatever your company does. Ive got great people skills and a GSOH and have a fantastic cv which im sending so that you can get back to me. At the end of the day you'll want someone who can think out of the box so if your firms got openings going let me know. Heres my cv, Im sure you'll like it!

Education: Past all my exams that I took, including GCSE, and got a top degree in Nuneaton social college where I did youth and sports studies.

Work experience: Great range of top placements including helping assistant manager

in local nightclub bar ~~and~~/work with government
office in plaᶜcing asylum seekers/and checking on
them. Have worked with customers in some big
stores ~~and~~/gained meaningful experience in inter-
personal relations and business/and am qualified
in top management issues and out of the box
thinking/ also work with Windows98.

Travel: Have travelled widely and been to
football clubs all over Europe and also Spanish
coasts or /costas/ and seen some really exotic
places in Thailand. Picked up enough Spanish
and other languages for good interpersonal
relations and have 24/7 attenᵗion-span. I'm great
with new ideas, and have a cool attitude if things
get hot, especially in a business situation. Also
like football and greyhounds and other top
sports. Played drums in school band so would be
good for your social oᶜcasions/

From an editorial in *The Times*, 4 August 2006/

Exercise 2

Visit Wells, England's ~~most~~ smallest city/ and
enjoy the wonderful cathedral with its famous
scissor arch, magnificent west Front, atmospheric
chatterhouse/ and knights who joust each
quarter/hour on the 14th century clock.

Explore the moated Bishop's Palace. Pevsner
described it as 'the most memorable in all
England.'

Walk in Vicars/ Close, one of the oldest streets
in Europe.

It is lived in now by vicars/ choral, Cathedral

=/ staff, and by boarders from near͜by Wells ∫)
   Cathedral school.

   Follow the stream of water from the Ⓦells #/
=/ flowing from the nineteenth Ⓒentury conduit #/
=/ ∫/ down the High street to another Ⓒhurch, St/ #/ ∂)
#/ Cuthbert's church itself often mistaken for the
   Ⓒathedral.

   If you walk alongside the curving moat you
⊃ₛ/ ∫) may see boy͜s and girl͜s from the Cathedral school, =/ ∫/
   which has been in existence for almost ⟨1,000⟩ ⟨spell out?⟩
� years. The school͜s motto is Esto Quod Es, and ⌐⌐/
=/ is latin for 'Be yourself,' or 'Be what you are.' ᴜ

From a tourist guide to Wells, Somerset, ∂)

Exercise 3

4 Ⓘ regard it as one of the best pleasures in Ⓛife to #/
   have a large glistening fish, straight out of the
⟨✓!?⟩ ⊂ depths of the sea and ⟨on to⟩ the charcoal in a perfect ᴜ
w/ island setting. My favorite fish for this purpose is
   the 'second category' fish, *melanouria* (saddled
r/ bream), a flat, fleshy, dark silvery fish with a black
ᴜ line down the length of its body, and ⟨skatharia⟩ ∿
)/ (black bream, very similar but even flatter than the
⌐ ⊃a/ melanouri, with a hint of golden rays on it.

Rena Salaman, *Greek Food* (Fontana, London, 1983), p. 213

Exercise 4

i/ It lies very low on the water, with only the small
4 hill of ⟨Cynthus⟩ to hold it from floating away. The
   blue and violet seas wash its shores, and the
   winds are fresh and sweet. In Ⓢpring it is a mass #/

of flowers, whole sheets of anemonones flooding
the meadows filled with gleaming columnsand
ruins glittering like bones. In summer it is
parched, with thistles and barleys growing thick
among the ruins, and in winter the winds of the
Agean pour over it, smoothing out the folds of
the draperies of the few remaining statues.

One should come to Delos on one one of those
transparent-blue mornings when the sea is very
still and the <u>meltemi</u> is blowing softly. One
should come leisurely in one of the black boats
belonging to the Naxian fisherman, whose skins
have turned to leather.

Robert Payne, *The Splendour of Greece* (Pan Books, London,
1964), p. 70/

Exercise 5

Zippy was a little wild. You could see it in her
eyes, the wildness of the heathland, even the
mysterious wetlands, yet they could also be ~~softl~~
softer than violet.

One night she bought Rick the Gypsy to the
bar. He was a young buck with a firm, toned
body. The DJ Was playing a record: [Are you
ready, are you ready for love, Yes I am, yes I
am.'/

Rick heard the words, then jumped up ready
to dance. He pulled girls to the dance/floor, and
anyone else too. He drank pints. Sweat streamed
down him. Rick pulled off his shirt. He danced
in the middle of the bar, crazily, exstatically,
occasionally shaddow-boxing an imaginary

punch bag. The sweat still ran on his broad back
and deep chest, healthy and tanned by the hottest
summer for at least one hundred years.
A crowd gathered, including the landlord, and
shaven-headed bouncers, expecting trouble, but
Rick kept on smiling, dancing, laughing, joking,
taunting a taut wire string of testosterone
energy. He danced like he had a dragon
scorching his feet too, but he just didn't care. He
was to alive to do anything else.

The author, *Hold Your Head Up High* (First English Books,
Poole, 2005), p. 386/7/

Exercise 6

One of your visits to Santorini must be to the
coast where good-tempered fishermen can be
seen sitting on the black volcanic sand drying or
mending their nets. There is happyness simply in
being near the sea, in watching the waves in the
sunshine, in breathing the fresh air, in the taste of
salt on your lips. Kamari and Perissa are not only
beautifull beaches/ but picturesque fishing
villages as well.

DURING the day fishing boats land there catch
of fresh fish, the fishermen bronzed and weather-
beaten, acustomed to hard/ship and peril. The
increase in tourism over the past ten year/ has
meant that fishermen have ben able to to keep
their nets, and more and more tavernas rely on
local fishermen to bring in their harvests from
the sea.

1 line # > ## Sandy Beaches

A new road now joins Phira to the sea. The best beaches, as mentioned above, are those of Perissa and Kammari. There you will find restaurants, tavernas and hotels from simple *pension* size to four-star luxury. In these seaside places the foothills of Mesa Vouno come down to the beach, and you can smell the scent of thyme and wild flowers from the hinterland.

You can feel the breeze coming off the open blue sea and fill your lungs deeply with sweet-smelling air. You can swim in the crystal-clear sea, then stretch out on the the black sand under the hot sun, or have a rest under the shade of Tamarisk trees. When it is time for lunch you can go to a nearby restaurant and be tempted by its succulent, freshly caught fish.

At Kamari there are several new and modern hotels which provide luxurious accommodation, but you may be equally happy renting an inexpensive room near the seaside, where the facilities are basic, but comfortable.

Perissa beach is also a wonderful place in the south of the island. It is a fine stretch of coastline—it's famous black sand made up of tiny particles of sand and stone. Perissa is blue sea, black sand, and blue skies, a formula that attracts thousands of visitors every year.

However some will lament the arrival of an airport large enough to handle big jets from all over the continent. There are restaurants and beachside tavernas where, after your swim, you can simply be lulled into a state of physical and mental relaxation, the warm blue sea only yards

away, a plate of black olivia, tomatos and fetta *ces/ e/*
cheese, sprinkled with oil and herbs; a glass of
cool white santorini Wine at your elbows *≠/ ⓘ*

Centuries ago a small Church was apparently
buried beneath the site of the present five-domed
church at Perissa. In 1835, a villager had a dream
that he should digging begin on the site, and so it
was that the old church was brought to light. In
a well nearby was found an Icon of the Panahgia
and a bronze Cross. Some villagers beleive even
to_jday that illness can be cured just by drinking
water from the well. Just behind the well is a
roman monument while near the feet of the *ⓧⓦf*
mountain can be found the ruins of an old
church (Santa Irini).

author? From Santorini – A Greek Island (First English Books, 2007), *δ/*

Notes

Exercise 1

There are no devious or cunning attempts to catch you
out in these exercises, unlike publishers' tests. Exercise 1,
which seems like the kind of CV many graduates *could*
actually write (without, I hope, being unfair) contains 43
basic errors. A copy-editor would have plenty to work on,
in addition (saying there are just 43 basic errors hides
those that would have been corrected by a copy-editor).
Whether or not the writer was justified in using lower case
in the subheading for CV cannot sensibly be questioned,
since a) it was a flippant piece, written by an editor at *The
Times*, pretending to be a student, and b) it could just be

house style, although that's highly unlikely. As you have been trained to follow the golden rule of consistency, why is cv acceptable but gsoh or gcse are not? So, award yourself an extra mark if you thought it should be CV.

Leader writers at *The Times* have such fun! They can get paid for writing spoof CVs. I like that kind of job.

Exercise 2

In this piece I've managed to find 35 errors. I admit to being keen on Wells, which is why this little piece is included. It's a medieval masterpiece of a tiny city a short distance from mystical Glastonbury. The proofreader I gave this piece to didn't pick up on 'scissor arch'; I suppose that's more a copy-editor's responsibility. The cathedral has more than one scissor arch; so, strictly, it must be 'arches'. [The proofreader soon gets to work on me. 'Yes,' she writes, 'but no one knows that unless they've been there. Even copy-editors would not be expected to pick this up. It's an author error.' You see how easy it is to pass the buck? Blame the poor author! Of course, she's right.]

There's also a problem of capitalisation in this piece. A local guidebook or pamphlet is always likely to give initial capitals to words like Cathedral, West Front and High Street but a book with a less parochial outlook would be prone to favour more use of lower case. The magnificent Chapterhouse in Wells, reached by a worn stone staircase, is just as wonderful as the West Front, so why capitals for West Front and not chapterhouse? Chapter House is another variant.

Looking at specific problems you'll encounter, let's start with paragraph 1, line 5: note '14th century clock'. Then, did you notice the inconsistency on the following page: 'nineteenth-century conduit'? You would have to check house style, and decide on one or the other or make it a query. Vicars' Close takes a possessive apostrophe but even definitive books on cathedral surroundings cannot decide if the singers, the Vicars Choral, need one. One is given here for consistency – hardly a good excuse, but good enough. Is it 'cathedral staff' or 'Cathedral staff'? You could argue that it should be 'Cathedral', as it is the specific, not the general. Ditto the next page, para 2, line 5.

'School' needs a capital S as it's part of the title (p. 185, para 3), ditto St Cuthbert's Church. Italics are clearly needed for the school's Latin motto.

Exercise 3

In this mini-exercise, there are just 9, at most 10 errors (including the word '*melanouri*'). In line 3 you'll find 'on to' corrected to 'onto', and that's correct because there is a sense of movement (see also page 134). However, it was 'on to' in the original, so that could be right too. [Now marked 'stet'.] The fish is not going to come 'straight out of the depths of the sea and onto the charcoal' in a single movement! Although corrected to 'onto' here, I think I prefer it as two words (and in any case, one should follow the original quotation).

The copy-editor correctly marked up 'melanouri' for italics, then added an 'a', to be consistent with line 5 (*melanouria*). This is actually how it was in the original (*melanouri*), published by a famous publishing house. It's either a mistake that was missed, or just possibly the author is referring to one fish; *melanouri* could be the singular, as in the Greek *paidi* (child) and *paidia* (children). It's easier here to pretend it's a mistake, and not intended, although one of those sneaky editors could plot such a trap in a publisher's test.

Exercise 4

There's nothing exceptional in this exercise; just the usual 'typos' and literals. The proofreader thought it was (line 1), low 'in' the water, as a boat lies *in* the water, but the author here had the idea of Delos almost floating *on* the surface, the island thought in mythical times to have been tethered by Zeus to the seabed with adamantine chains, to stop it floating away. (He [the author] is correct with 'lies . . . in the water' – 'lays' would refer to laying an egg.)

[I hope I'm correct because I've since lost the book. I can't really remember whether it should be low 'in' or 'on' the water. Help! You can get into deep water and deeper sweats for such small mistakes.]

There's no reason to italicise the hill on Delos known as Cynthus (or Kynthos). Foreign place names are not italicised just because they are 'foreign' – e.g. Place de la Concorde, Notre Dame, Montmartre.

A common mistake is to capitalise the seasons. The *Meltemi* is italicised here but it can be in roman (house style). It's more usual to have an initial capital (but there's no fixed rule). The *Meltemi*, a summer wind, can gust hard but when it blows softly it can be as gentle as an English zephyr, balmy as the west wind. *New ODWE* goes for 'meltemi', roman, no initial capital (the same for 'harmattan', the dry wind from the Sahara that blows towards the West African coast).

The total number of errors to find is 15.

Exercise 5

If you look hard, you can find 22 errors in this exercise. Again, it's easy. In paragraph one, line 3, the proofreader had crossed out 'soft', so it read 'they could also be softer than violet'. It's not easy when reading blind. Having written the book myself, I know I missed out only a comma.

The error that was corrected to lower case (gypsy) is questionable as an error, if this was the man's title – Rick the Gypsy.

That summer was glorious (2003); you may remember it. Burning days of lush sunshine, warm nights. Eva and Archie in the same bed would soon have thrown off the bedclothes!

[There was an extra sentence here but the proofreader wrote in the margin of the proofs, 'The addition is completely incomprehensible to me – sorry!' Once again, she's spot on. You cannot allow emotions to interfere with your work. The addition would have been something like this: *'Look, Eva, I know you're very attractive but there's work to be done. And Archie needs some new clothes!'* It's got nothing to do with proofreading, and should therefore be deleted. I hope I can slip it in here anyway, when the proofreader isn't looking!]

Exercise 6

This exercise is a little more demanding. In a 'real' set of proofs, do remember you could read five or more pages and discover nothing. The number of errors is 58. By now, you should be finding them easily. You wouldn't be expected to know or check the spelling of Greek place names (for example, Kamari and Perissa) but in a test you'd at least have to query any inconsistencies.

Note the need to lose a line at the end of the first paragraph, and begin a new paragraph. (However, this is also a questionable error without a house style guide but at least you would notice other indented paragraphs later on.)

There's no need to italicise 'tavernas' (too well known as small Greek restaurants).

The heading on page 188 needs a line space above and below (but you couldn't be expected to know this without the typescript or house style guidance). Mark up the second word (Beaches) in bold. A common style for subtitles is two full line spaces above the subtitle and one full line space below.

No hyphen is needed (paragraph 2, last line), 'freshly caught fish'. As soon as you see a word ending in -*ly*, it usually denotes an adverb, and a hyphen is not necessary in this kind of construction.

Don't forget a comma (p. 188, last paragraph, line 1) is always required after however – except in such constructions as, 'However you look at it . . .'

On page 189, you might question whether there is a trade name involved (and therefore initial capitals required) – is it Santorini White or Cool White? Also, if 'santorini' were a grape variety, it could be lower case, upper case for a manufacturer of the wine. Actually, it's none of these, so no need to worry! (Incidentally, the style of marking up for initial caps in this exercise includes a capital letter above the three lines in the margin – this is just to make it easier to see. You could just use three lines, and dispense with the capital letter.)

It's pretty hard to have a glass of wine 'at your elbows', unless either your elbows are very close together on the table, or you have two glasses of wine, one for each elbow! You might query if this should be 'elbow'. (A sharp-eyed copy-editor will then say that this might imply the person is disabled and has only one elbow . . .)

Did you spot the wrong font on the same page, paragraph 2 line 10, 'monument'? It's easy enough to mark up.

The style for the references is a standard format; in this case the house style is without full points. You could not have known this without a style sheet so you would have either to mark up for full points or delete them (as I did) and better still, query if one or the other *is* the house style. The last reference does not follow the style of previous examples for books so you need to have noticed that. There is also no place of publication reference for First English Books, and should the author's name be mentioned in Exercise 5? (Count as 2 errors.)

The 'total' number of errors you could have found in the six exercises is 183.

- If you were within five to ten of that number (183–74), well done, an excellent effort!
- Between 173 and 168 is only fair.
- If you scored less than 168, you definitely need more practice!

Too stressed out with your performance? Try the exercises again, and see how much you improve! Make a mental note to visit Santorini one day, and discover the magic of the island for yourself.

There's much more to learn in the full set of proofs, uncorrected proofs and corrected proofs with personal scorecard, all available only from the website at www.pocketbookofproofreading.co.uk.

* * *

In October 2006, Archie was temporarily confined in a kind of museum – the Bodleian Library in Oxford, founded in 1602 by Oxonian Sir Thomas Bodley. This was an exhibition to commemorate the centenary of the birth of Archie's owner, Sir John Betjeman. It was apparently, in terms of visitor numbers, the Bodleian's most successful ever exhibition. So many people came to see Archie – he was a real hit.

I've no idea where he is now. One Spanish-sounding lady at the Bodleian thought that Archie had been 'locked away downstairs in a big room' after the exhibition but the curator informed me just before Christmas that Archie had gone back to his owner. She couldn't tell me who that was, or even where he [Archie] was, in case word of Archie's whereabouts ever got out, and someone tried to steal him.

If you google Archie, he gets only 1,410 hits but Eva Longoria, perhaps shooting the next series of *Desperate Housewives*, returns a more respectable 3,500,000.

Talking about Christmas in the previous paragraph but one, and having just listened to Welsh soloist Kathryn Jenkins singing, 'Have Yourself A Merry Little Christmas', I'm speechless. Kathryn Jenkins manages only 999,000 hits, and I can hear Eva saying, '*Muh!*' Or, '*I told you so!*'

My excuse was imagining that Archie could do with some company – if not Eva and Kathryn, how about friends like the BBC news presenter Emily Maitlis or Connie Fisher, the new star of revamped *The Sound of Music*? I think I planned the idea of introducing Archie, Eva, and others to annoy (subconsciously and unfairly) the proofreader. It's as if I were waiting for her to say, 'For heaven's sake, you're supposed to be writing a little book about proofreading!'

One problem is that I've been working on this book for too long now. It must be almost a year but you still have to get the facts right. Truthfully, I don't really care *that* much about Eva et al. but I do worry when I think about Archie in a box somewhere, locked away from the world, and with no one to console or anthropomorphically hug him.

Facts (accurate ones) are always so important, whether you're an editor, copy-editor or proofreader. For example, when Betjeman was dying on a bed in Cornwall in 1984, he was actually clutching both Archie (see p. 84) *and*

'Jumbo', a toy elephant, one in each hand. Archie seems to me like a kind of monolithic throwback, a desperately individual bear, a most extraordinary character.

If you look closely at Archie, you start thinking about cruelty to animals – Jumbo's in the same state. What a magnificent pair!

Archie even has his own Wikipedia entry. The stuffed bear is given tribute in Betjeman's work, *Summoned by Bells*. He wrote: 'The only constant, sitting there, patient and hairless, is a bear.'

Wouldn't it be nice if the executors of the late Poet Laureate, or the photographer, would allow me to publish a picture of Archie! How much money would that cost? It could be a very long time before he's ever seen in public again. I guess I could ask them. I'll give the space below a title, ARCHIE, just in case they say, 'Yes'.

Note: make sure you read carefully through the Addenda. Here you'll find what proofreader Michèle kindly describes as 'the really good value of the Addenda with a Schott-like miscellany of goodies in it'. What follows is a foretaste – a kind of 'squeezed in' mini-addenda.

- Glance back to pages 23 and 24 now, and see if you can find a typesetting error. It's in the list of words that should 'always be spelt -ise'. Award yourself a huge pat on the back if you have already spotted this. To be in the right order, as the page is 'split', part of the column on page 24 with the words 'despise, devise, disguise, excise' should be transposed or taken back to page 23, and swapped for 'prise, reprise, revise, and supervise', which ought to be on page 24. The four words need to go in at 'exercise', which must move down!
- On page 69 (at pre-decimalisation money), someone also noted the expression 5/6 for 5 shillings and 6 pence, seen on veg etc. on a stall, along with 2/6 – for 2 shillings and six pence, or half a crown. [Sorry, that should be 6 pence.]
- On page 74, you can also have bons mots as a plural, as well as bon mots. Proofreader Michèle pointed this out, as seen in her

Oxford English Dictionary (OED). However, on page 71, it does say: 'The lists that follow represent the preference of *one* particular publisher only.' Preferences in house style can even extend to preferred plurals, so I've chosen not to add 'bons mots' to the actual list.

- On page 77, last line, Michèle rightly comments in the margin, 'Not sure why you've used [ ] here as an aside or comment as you haven't necessarily done so before. Do check [ ] thru'out.' There's a note about this in the Addenda on page 230. I used to love writing query notes to in-house editors, ones where you could write: 'Do please check . . .' Let them do the work! I'm afraid I don't have the time now after 15 months to whiz through the typescript looking for [ ] and ( ).

- On page 96, Michèle (just had to stop a second to paste in grave accent) remarks in margin of proofs that some of the columns in Table 1.2 don't add up! 'Should they?' she blithely adds. The answer: the columns should add up (columns 1 and 4 do; 2, 3 and 5 don't). Michèle is just being a good proofreader. She doesn't have to worry about the actual figures; the author would need to scurry off and check figures, then provide a satisfactory explanation or the correct numbers.

- On page 116, you could also add to third bullet copy, 'and names of people who worked on the book'.

- On page 131, line 11. Note that not all corrections have an oblique added after a correction. Use an oblique (/) for every change that is *not* an insertion or deletion.

- Page 160, two lines up from bottom of page: '10 pages per hour'. Cf. 'about ten pages per hour', last line of page 163. Choose which is right, according to house style. This mistake (inconsistency) was left in – in the belief that seeing such errors 'in print' may help you to improve your proofreading skills. There's another good example on page 164, line 3.

- On page 227 of the Addenda, you'll find a reference to the blank space left for Archie's photo. This has now been taken up by this mini-addenda.

Just as I reach the end of this section, Word is asking me to correct 'this' to 'these', as I've used 'addenda' and not the singular 'addendum'. To stop myself going on further still or, as I heard a non-native English speaker say last week, 'going off at a tandem', when she meant 'going off at a tangent', I'm finding the easy way out.

I have succumbed to a page-120 feeling (see that page, pages 227–8 and page 231). I can't take any more!

'Archie'

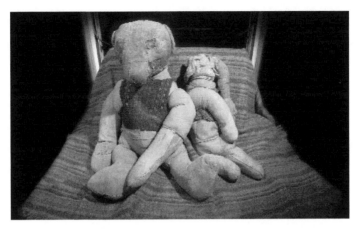

'Oh, Archie,' I can hear John Betjeman saying, 'does it have to end like this?'

Photo of Archibald Ormsby-Gore reproduced courtesy of The Times/Leon Neal, NI Syndication, and with permission from the Betjeman estate

and Eva

Would she like Archie too?

Photo of Eva Longoria reproduced courtesy of The Times/Chris Harris and NI Syndication

Glossary

Use this brief glossary to familiarise yourself with some publishing terms. It is not essential to know all of them but it will help you to understand a little more about the publishing industry.

accents   If you are adding an accent to a letter, strike through the unaccented letter, then write in the margin the letter and accent. The copy-editor has correctly pencilled in the margin here: 'This isn't a definition of accents.' She is absolutely right, of course, but this isn't the place to start explaining the meaning of acute, circumflex, grave accents, *et al.* (There's room only for one. The 'acute' in acute accent derives from *acuere*, to sharpen, and *acus*, needle. A recherché observation? Of course.)

acknowledge-ments   Statement by the author of a book acknowledging the use of material by other authors.

Arabic numerals   1, 2, 3, 4, 5, 6, 7, 8, 9, 0. Compare with Roman numerals i, ii, iii, iv, v, vi, vii, viii, ix, x, etc., which are often used in the preliminary pages (prelims) of a book.

appendix   Separate, additional or supplementary material added (appended) at the end of a book, and which forms (part of) the end-matter (plural: appendices).

artwork   Any of the matter in graphic form used in a book, such as figures, tables, or drawings of one kind or another. (Copy-editors may write in margin, *Insert a/w here*, a/w being a fairly common abbreviation for artwork. The proofreader must make sure the artwork is in the right place, if ready, and check captions and titles.)

author–date system   Also known as the *Harvard System*. A system of referencing often used in scientific, technical and medical books, when the author wishes to refer to references in the text. Just the name (of author) and year of publication are given (these are known as parenthetical references). No superscript numbers are used. example: *Numbers of cuckoos are declining (Jolly, 2004) in their western habitat.*

bibliography   A full list of books chosen by an author, usually relevant to the particular text. Compare with a *Select Bibliography*, which lists only a limited selection of books used as source material, and/or that are relevant to the text.

BSI   British Standards Institution, responsible (*inter alia*) for introducing BS 5261C:2005 (marks for copy preparation and proof correction).

Butcher, Judith   If Lynne Truss is the 'Punctuation Queen', Judith Butcher is the 'Editing Queen'. First honorary president of the SfEP, famous author of *Copy-editing: The Cambridge Handbook*. The fourth edition is recommended for copy-editors and proofreaders.

bracket   A square bracket [ ] is typically used for an interpolation/comment in the text by the author; compare with *parenthesis*. A brace – { } – may be used to enclose two or more lines.

capitalisation   Less of a problem now than it was for the Victorians, who capitalised words more or less at will. In general, capitals are discouraged; when in doubt use lower case. Do not capitalise words that denote important, wondrous, uplifting things.

caps (also cap)   Abbreviation for capitals/capital letters. Compare with s.c. (small caps).

caption   The words used in a figure or table to describe what is shown. Purists might say that a table has a title but a figure has a caption.

cf.　　　　　　The meaning of the abbreviation *cf.* is 'compare', from the Latin *confer*.

chapter head　Another name for a chapter title.

character　　　In printing, any single letter, numeral, etc.

collating
proofs/
collation　　　Originally, this was the examination and comparison of texts/statements in order to note points of agreement and disagreement. In publishing, from an editorial viewpoint, the term means checking an already marked set of proofs, and adding/deleting to/from this set the author's as well as any further corrections from the proofreader's set.

colophon　　　A publisher's emblem or logo.

commission-
ing editor　　An editor responsible for the commissioning of a book, from its inception through to eventual production.

consistency　　A golden rule for copy-editors and proofreaders. Achieve it.

contents　　　Found in the *prelims*, listing the chapters or divisions of a book.

copy　　　　　In proofreading context, matter to be reproduced as text; also written matter or text in books, as distinct from graphic material.

dedication	An inscription in a book to honour a relative or friend. A dedication is more likely to be found at the beginning of a book, in the prelim pages, whereas an *epigraph* may be a quotation found at the beginning of a chapter.
design memo	Another name for style sheet.
design treatment	Name for matter or material that may need to be the subject of attention from the design department.
dia(e)resis	A mark placed over the second of two adjacent vowels to indicate it is to be pronounced separately, e.g. *daïs, Danaë, Citroën*
display	A copy-editing term of instruction used to indicate that material should be indented (separated or distinguished in some way) from the main body of the text. Quotations over a certain length are usually 'marked up' for display.
double-spaced	Authors submitting manuscripts should always ensure they are typed/printed double-spaced (handily leaving enough space for the copy-editor).
electronic sources	Internet documents, videos, email messages, web pages, URLs, articles in online journals, etc.

elision
Properly speaking, the omission of a syllable or vowel at the beginning or end of a word, or the omission of parts of a book. In proofreading, elision is often used to indicate the shortening of page numbers, chapters or ranges of dates in years (as in decades), such as pp. 157–9 or 157–59 rather than pp. 157–159. (*En rules* are normally used for eliding dates and pairs of numbers.)

ellipsis
A series of three dots used to indicate the omission of part of a text, extract, or quotation. The plural is *ellipses*.

em/em rule
A printer's term used to indicate length, or in this case the width of the letter 'M'. How wide this actually is depends on the *font* used (e.g. Times New Roman, Ariel, Verdana) and also on the *point size* (12pt, 24pt, 36pt, 72pt, etc.) An em rule is a rule (a solid horizontal line) of that length.

en/en rule
Also a printer's term, this being a rule half the size or length of an em rule. Spaced en rules are normally used now for parenthetical dashes. In the US, however, closed-up em rules (no space either side of dash) are the norm (for dashes).

endmatter
Whatever copy or matter that follows on from the main part or text of a book. Endmatter may consist of references, a bibliography, an index, etc.

endnotes   Notes made by the author, found either at
                  the end of each chapter, or at the end of
                  the book.

epigraph   An introductory quote intended to reflect
                  the theme of what follows. A quotation at
                  the beginning of a book, chapter, etc.

et al.   Often used in notes and references,
                  meaning 'and others' (when there are too
                  many authors' names to mention). Not
                  usually in italics but occasionally so in
                  bibliographies. Cf. 'inter alia', among
                  others. The incredibly observant might
                  find an inconsistency in the italic and
                  roman use of et al. in this book!

extract   Normally a quotation in a book that
                  becomes an extract because it is displayed
                  in the text, either by being indented from
                  the main text (to make it stand out), or
                  by being set in a smaller point size.

flag   A device, such as a piece of coloured paper,
                  attached to individual folio(s), or pages, of
                  a typescript to make such pages, or matter
                  within those pages, easier to locate (e.g. for
                  the insertion of artwork), i.e. 'flagged up'.

folio   Originally, *inter alia*, a sheet of paper
                  folded in half to make two leaves for a
                  book (from Latin, *folium*, leaf). In
                  publishing, consider it as a very grand
                  name for a page in a book. Pages of a

typescript are also referred to as 'folios'. The abbreviation *ff.* means either 'folios', or 'and the following pages/lines', etc.

follow on
Instruction used by a copy-editor to tell the typesetter not to leave any space or extra space where indicated. The author may, for example, have printed or typed out a page (or folio) where the page length or depth is too short, or much shorter than usual, making it appear, for example, like a section break (when none was intended). So, the copy-editor draws a connecting line between the spaced out text, and will write 'Follow on', encircling the written instruction.

font
A complete set of type of one style and (point) size. 'Fount' is an older word that meant the same. 'Font' is more common in the US. See also *fount*.

footnote
A note printed at the bottom of a page, to which attention is usually drawn by a mark (often a superscript or indicator) in the text.

fount
UK word for *font*, but getting a little archaic. *The Times* changed its fount in 2006, 'blending Times New Roman with Times Modern'.

foreword
A word that often causes the novice proofreader to stumble, as it gets mixed

up with 'forward'. It is an introduction to
a book, usually *not* written by the author
(see also *preface*).

freelance   A self-employed person, usually a writer
or artist, hired for specific assignments. In
medieval Europe, a mercenary soldier or
adventurer. Also called freelancer.

fresh page   Instruction used by the copy-editor to tell
the typesetter to start a new page, which
may be a *verso* (left) page or *recto* (right)
page. The copy-editor, for example may
write, 'Begin fresh page here', encircling
the instruction in the usual way. It's not
always *that* obvious to an author, to start
or continue text on a new (fresh) page.
Authors and translators are not expected
to copy-edit their own work, so there will
always be difficulties of one kind or
another to resolve.

full out   Flush to the margin, usually the left one,
and not indented.

full point   The full stop (US: period).

galley proof   A proof taken before the text is made up
into pages. Very old-fashioned nowadays.

**half-title
page**   The short title of a book, printed on the
right-hand page (*recto* page), and always
preceding the *title page*.

Harvard system	The Harvard system of referencing (a way to treat references in a book) is very similar to the *author–date system*. No superscript numbers are used. Author's name is given in the text, together with year of publication, and page reference, if any. Contrast with the *numbered note system* or Vancouver system.
house style	The idiosyncrasies of each publishing house, when translated onto the page. The preferred style of presentation and usage of each publisher. For (a random) example, preferring a priori and a posteriori to be in roman and not italics, or vice versa.
ibid.	Latin for 'in the same place', abbreviation for *ibidem*. Referring to a book, etc. previously cited (used in notes). Frivolously, *The Left Handed Dictionary* (Collier Books, New York, 1963) describes 'Ibid.' as a) a prolific writer of quotations (no relation to Ovid or Avid); and b) a famous Latin poet. (Ibid.)
idem	Latin, 'the same'. Used to refer to an article, chapter, etc. previously cited.
imprimatur	'Let it be printed.' Approval or sanction for something to be printed.
imprint	A name for a publishing house, under which it trades or carries on business

(publishes). 'Touchstone' is an imprint of Simon & Schuster.

imprint page A page containing information about a publisher and the publishing history of a book, found on the left (*verso*) page after the *title page*. Will include CIP [cataloguing] data, ISBN, copyright notice, etc. Also called title page verso.

ISBN Abbreviation for International Standard Book Number, a unique coding number allotted to every published book.

justify A term in printing meaning to adjust spaces between words in a line of type so it is the right length, or adjusted so that the line of type fits exactly; making left and right ends of lines align. A copy-editor or proofreader may mark up text to be justified.

landscape A table or figure set out 'lengthwise', or sideways, cf. *portrait*.

l.c. Abbreviation for lower case.

ligature Not an instrument of torture you'd like to apply to a publisher's neck for not giving you enough work, but a character of two or more joined letters, e.g. æ.

literal(s) Literals are misspellings or misprints in the text (from late Latin *litteralis*, concerning letters).

loc. cit.   Latin for 'in the place cited'. Used in
            notes. Abbreviation for *loco citato*.

long page   A page that is not of the correct *page
            depth*, simply too many lines.

lower case   Lower case letters are small letters. Seasons,
            for example, are lower case: spring, autumn.

manuscript   Originally something written by hand as
            opposed to being printed. The original
            work of an author, whether written or
            typed, as submitted for publication.
            Nowadays, mostly called a typescript.

marginal   Proofreading marks made in the margin
mark(s)   to signify or amplify the meaning of an
            instruction to the typesetter in the text.
            Marginal marks are divided between left
            and right margins as they occur, the order
            being (in both margins) from left to right.

marked   A set of proofs that has had corrections
proofs   added to it by the proofreader.

numbered   A system of numbered notes for biblio-
note system   graphical references, often used in social
            science and humanities titles. References
            are usually placed at the end of each
            chapter, sometimes together at the end of
            the book. Superscript numbers in the text
            (indicators) are used to number the
            references in the appropriate place.

oblique (stroke)	Another name for *solidus*. Thus: / The humble oblique stroke or slash has lately come to prominence because BS 5261C: 2005 requires it to be used 'after every change that is not an insertion or deletion'.
op. cit.	Latin for 'in the work cited'. Used in notes. Abbreviation for *opere citato*.
original(s)	Anything that is not a copy of something. In publishing, a piece of artwork, whether pasted up or not, as supplied by author.
orphan	The first line of a new paragraph that happens to fall on the last line of a page of text (cf. *widow*).
page depth	The extent of print within the margins on a printed page, from top to bottom.
page proofs	Proofs produced after galley proofs; separate, numbered pages.
pagination	The numbering in sequence of the pages in a typescript or book.
parenthesis	Round brackets, ( ), plural: parentheses. See also *bracket*.
passim	Latin for 'here and there'. Used to indicate that what is referred to occurs frequently/throughout the work cited.

point size   A unit of measurement in printing; the size of any type style (8pt Verdana, 12pt Times New Roman, etc.) There are about 72 points to the inch.

portrait   'Upright' table, figure, or illustration (cf. *landscape*).

preface   An introductory section to a book, typically written by the author (cf. *foreword*).

prelims/ preliminary pages   All the pages in a book *before* the main text begins (title page, contents page[s], dedication page, etc.). Also called front matter.

proofreading marks   The most appropriate set of marks to use for copy preparation and proof correction can be found in BS 5261C:2005. To the uninitiated, they can look like mere squiggles.

quotes/ quotation marks   In the UK, the custom is 'single quotes but "double" within single'.

q.v.   An abbreviation for *quod vide*, 'which see', often used in notes and references.

quotations   Quotations in a text are often subject to specific design treatment. Quotations over a certain number of words (usually 40 or over) may be displayed. If so, opening and closing quotes are not used.

ragged right	Type where the right-hand edge is not justified right or aligned but left 'ragged' (as in these glossary entries).
range left/ right	An instruction to align lines of type to the left (or right as in 'range right')
recto	The right-hand (and odd numbered) page(s) of a book.
references	An author's sources used in the writing of a book; listed at the end of each chapter, or end of book.
rule	A (solid) line used in printing; various lengths.
run on	A copy-editing instruction. Do not start a new line/new paragraph. Run one line on (close up) to the next, without a section break/new line.
running head(s)	Words at the top of *verso* and *recto* pages (but not chapter starts), indicating book title, name of author, chapter title, and so on. A fairly common form is: book title, *verso*, chapter title, *recto*.
select bibliography	Where the sources listed are partial or selected.
serial comma(s)	Serial commas are used in lists of items. For example: 'the colours indigo, turquoise, and violet' (cf: 'the colours indigo, turquoise and violet'.) Serial commas are

used much more in the US. It's often a matter of house style as to which is chosen. It doesn't matter which, if you aren't given guidance, but do be consistent. Often known as the Oxford comma.

SfEP   The Society for Editors and Proofreaders. Originally called the Society of Freelance Editors and Proofreaders.

short page   A page where the *depth* is too short; too few lines.

short-title system   The practice of referring to a reference in short form after first (full) mention; citing an abbreviated form of reference for second and subsequent mentions.

(*sic*)   Latin for 'so' or 'thus'. Often in italics, in square or round brackets. Used to indicate that what may be read as odd or questionable in a text is in fact accurate. e.g. 'The Queen Mother allegedly once drank two pints (*sic*) of gin before breakfast.' It shows that quoted words, even if unlikely, are correctly reproduced. An example from *Celebrity Big Brother*: Jade Goody, by her own account, reckons she is 'the most 25th inferlential [sic] person in the world'. Use square brackets to enclose [*sic*] for any interpolation(s) by author. *Sic* should not be used to sneer or scoff at 'unintentional error or illiteracy'.

small caps   Small capital letters. Abbreviation: s.c.
                     Small caps are typically used for BC/AD
                     dates and compass points, really a matter
                     of house style.

solidus   See *oblique.*

sort   Any of the individual characters making
                     up a font; a character or letter.

special   Any unusual character or letter; term also
sort(s)   used in a *style sheet* to draw attention of
                     typesetter (e.g. ∑, ‡, ‰). Special sorts
                     include foreign language characters, maths
                     symbols, etc. In electronic editing, these
                     would be tagged.

spread   If you open a book, the left and right
                     pages together constitute a spread.

stet   Instruction to typesetter to ignore or
                     cancel a change called for by the copy-
                     editor or proofreader. Latin for 'let it
                     stand'. A mark or word indicating that
                     deleted matter should be retained (i.e. left
                     as it was before the attempted correction).
                     No longer used in BS 5261C:2005.

style sheet   Usually made by a copy-editor (and/or
                     supplied by in-house editor to proof-
                     reader). A list for reference and clarity
                     describing house style points, and any
                     special sorts.

subscript	A smaller size (sized down) character or letter printed below the base line, in 'inferior' position, e.g. H_2O *is the chemical formula for water.*
superscript	A (smaller size) character or letter printed above the line in 'superior' position. Superscripts are used as 'indicators' for references, e.g. *Jolly* [23] *has written extensively on the declining habitat of the cuckoo.*
textual mark(s)	Mark in the text made by the proofreader to indicate to typesetter the exact place to which the instruction refers.
title page	A *recto* page in the prelims of a book giving the full book title.
typescript	Formerly any typewritten material as opposed to handwritten material (manuscript). Now it means any copy, whether typed, printed out from a PC, or on a disk, as supplied to the publisher/typesetter by the author.
typesetting	The setting of type by a typesetter.
typo(s)	Mistakes made by the typesetter. Whereas *literals* are misspellings or misprints in the text, a *typo* or typographical error is, for example, setting type in the wrong point size, or style, or making a page too long or too short, etc.

u.c.   Abbreviation for upper case.

upper case   CAPITAL letters.

verso   The left-hand page(s) of a book, bearing the even numbers. Plural: versos. Cf. *recto*

w.f.   Abbreviation for wrong font/fount.

widow   The last line of a paragraph that carries over to the first line of a new page.

word break   A word break is made when a hyphen is inserted to divide a word at the end of a (justified) line of type. 'Bad' word breaks are to be avoided.

Addenda

Here's a tiny (started small but grew) list of things that could have been added but weren't. It's not in exact 'chronological', i.e. page order, but jumps about here and there. You have to draw the line somewhere, or the book would not have been finished, more widows and orphans would have been born, and the indexer would have had to cope with changed pagination.

If you feel like adding anything, or you have some particular points worth mentioning, please do send them to the email address below, so that they can be added to *The Pocket Book of Proofreading*'s website. All contributions are welcome!

- Quote marks over one or more paragraphs in *non-displayed material*. Note that end quotes are not used for each paragraph ending, until the final paragraph. Below is (another) ridiculously long example to show you how it works – this from Joseph Conrad's *Heart of Darkness*. You'd expect a closing quote at 'after'. This is an unusual example, however. Any quote this long would normally be set out, without quotes, but this is how it looks in Conrad's novel (apart from the ending quotation mark after 'darkness', which has been added).

'Now when I was a little chap I had a passion for maps. I would look for hours at South America, or Africa, or Australia, and lose myself in all the glories of exploration. At that time there were many blank spaces on the earth, and when I saw one that looked particularly inviting on a map (but they all look that) I would put my finger on it and say, When I grow up I will go there . . . But there was one yet – the biggest, the most blank, so to speak – that I had a hankering after.

'True, by this time it was not a blank space any more. It had got filled since my boyhood with rivers and lakes and names. It had ceased to be a blank space of delightful mystery – a white patch for a boy to dream gloriously over. It had become a place of darkness . . .'

- On page 47, mention is made of square brackets inside parentheses. Another example is when a book published a long time ago has a later edition, so an author might choose in a citation to put the original date of publication in square brackets, this followed by the date of publication of the edition used by the author, hence (Darwin [1859] 2005).

- The website designer of the *Pocket Book of Proofreading* (Bart Nagel) wishes to add: 'On reading page 69 I wanted to clarify that, although all domain names are case-insensitive, the file system of the server may not be (Linux/Unix file systems are, Windows ones aren't); and so whatever.com/Index.html may be different to whatever.com/index.html.

- Bart also commented: 'On page 38 you say to include a comma before "etc." if more than one term precedes, but then on page 43 you include one before the "etc." following "HOWS MY DRIVING. . ." even though that's the only term. [I had to remove the comma.] I laughed out loud at your mention of chavs, but shortly after was confused about the point of the little ramble about *Desperate Housewives*. Maybe that's just because I don't watch the show.' [I don't watch it that much either but Eva Longoria is, well, she's 'attractive'. I know the idea of pairing her off with Archie is a bit gloopy, but it's just my idea of fun. No harm's done either way. Archie is incapable of having any influence on Eva – on to or onto – it makes no difference. As for the merits of on to and onto, here's one example that might help: 'He struggled on to victory' is clearly not the same as, 'He struggled onto victory.']
- A typical web reference might be (endnotes): http://www.biota.org/people/douglasadams/index.html
- A web article from a newspaper: http://www.guardian.co.uk/Archive/Article/ 0,5673,563618,00.html
- Example of a reference in a journal, this taken from the *New Scientist*: 'In one case researchers saw a chimp remove a dead bushbaby and consume it (*Current Biology*, DOI: 10.1016/j.cub.2006.12.042).' [DOI stands for 'Digital Object Identifier'. A DOI is 'a unique string created to identify a piece of intellectual property in an online environment'. Over 25 million DOIs have been registered so

far. This is technical and is best explained at www.crossref.org. As a proofreader, you don't have to worry about such references because, in the unlikely (but also quite possible) event of meeting them, a house style guide ought to be provided, and the copy-editor should have already checked them.]

- An example of a non sequitur seen on a sealed pack of Tesco cut daffodils: 'Lilies can be harmful to cats if eaten.'

- A recent example of *sic* (thus): 'Disgraced President Robert Mugabe said it was acceptable to bash (*sic*) his MDC opposition party opponents.'

- An example of inconsistency: there are ten uses of 'spelled' in *The Pocket Book of Proofreading*, nine out of ten are the phrasal verb, to spell out. There are six uses of 'spelt' (only one is 'spelt out'). It was decided to let this inconsistency stand, and just point it out in the Addenda.

- On page 95, can you see anything 'wrong' with the source note for Figure 2.1? That remarkable creation, the en rule, is missing between the A and the Z. What you are looking at is a mere hyphen.

- Sign seen on a *Roadliner* bus, above the exhaust pipe: 'Danger – hot gasses'. Perhaps the bus was imported from the US, where spelling 'gases' as 'gasses' is the norm?

- Copy-editors editing on-screen often use the Track Changes facility, found under Tools in Word. Changes made by the copy-editor and/or author can be highlighted and/or modified, and either accepted or rejected. It's a useful 'gizmo' for copy-editors.

- The remark on page 107 about handwritten marks needs qualifying. These were originally hand-drawn but then Bart demonstrated his technical wizardry, producing 'vector-based' marks. It's like they were hand-drawn, if you see what I mean, but actually they're not!
- The proofreader makes a useful observation about page 116, line 2. This has been staring me in the face for months, and was always missed. [Like this cliché, 'staring me in the face'. How shall I get round this, in modern parlance? 'Like I was looking at it, full on'?] She writes in the latest list of queries: 'First paragraph, roman vs Arabic. Is this OK? OUP has Roman for numerals, roman for font. Weird.' A quick check in *New ODWE* confirms this. Type of a plain upright kind used in ordinary print is 'roman' but 'Roman' denotes the alphabet used for English and most other European languages. It will be hurriedly changed to 'Roman numerals'.
- On page 129, line 14: note that (book) titles (normally italic) are here set in roman because the quotation itself is in italic.
- On page 133, last paragraph, there is mention of 'none' and its use with singular/plural verbs. You *can* use a plural form of a verb with the singular pronoun 'none'. It just depends on context but this example is 'cheating' a little, since the noun is plural. For example: 'The solicitor left millions but seemingly no children (none are mentioned in his will).'
- In *The Pocket Book of Proofreading*, you might think that the proofreading marks are a

little on the small side [Bart is such a neat worker!]. In practice, your marks, when you are marking up copy, are likely to be bigger, and there's no harm in that. Don't try to make your own marks minimalist just because they could be construed as such in this book.

- The proofreader has found a mystery that perplexed many readers of the original Freelance MS course. On page 36, she noted that she 'can't see the difference really between "a small, oblong table" and "a short yellow minidress"'. Am I just being thick?' Many people asked the same question. I just think it's worth leaving in because it's so ridiculously perplexing, and I'm not too sure of the answer! The answer, I believe, is that 'oblong' and 'table' are not jointly modified by 'small' but 'yellow' and 'minidress' are jointly modified by 'short'. Yet, I don't yet understand how 'yellow' can be modified by 'short', but no doubt it's all to do with 'joint' modification. How about: 'a small, square bikini', and 'a small yellow bikini'?

- The proofreader also wants to know the answer to this query: 'On page 38, comma after "etc." if followed by phrase such as "and so forth". Would one actually say "etc., and so forth"?' I think it means, if after 'etc.' you tack on some inconsequential little phrase, almost as an afterthought, afterwards, then a comma is needed.

'Tears rolled down Archie's cheeks. He'd been locked away in the Bodleian for so long that his tears had collected an admixture of sand, dust and grime, etc., but little else.'

'Tears rolled down Archie's cheeks. He'd been locked away in the Bodleian for so long that his tears had collected an admixture of sand, dust and grime, etc. and his mouth had been dry for eleven years, ever since his master removed the whisky.'

The proofreader comments: 'Just to put a spanner in the works, I would put a comma after "etc." in the second sentence illustrating "etc." because the previous phrase "sand, dust and grime" has an "and" in it, so the next "and" needs a comma before it. Hey ho!' It's terrible what one does to try to prove a point. I capitulate here but have you noticed the sly little entry I make, some lines further down at 'My final reason. . .'?

● On page 39, Bart has provided his own, very personal smileys. One has a lop-sided grin; the other looks odd, as if trying to be grumpy but not really succeeding. Bart wondered if smileys should be used here. ('I think I'd show them as colons and parentheses rather than as pictures since we're talking about them in terms of colon usage.') You can see how difficult it can be to get editors, authors, copy-editors and proof-readers to agree – on anything! If you have any personal likes or dislikes regarding usage and abusage of the English language, please do send them to the email address given. They'll either be posted on the website and/or be published in future editions of *The Pocket Book of Proofreading*. (We are such a diverse nation, often obsessed with trivia and idiosyncrasies, and I know there'll be a fair number sent in.)

- Postcodes (see page 150). The exception to the rule about placing a postcode under the name of a town or city is London. It's usual, for example, to see: London E98 1XY, on the same line.

- On page 151, proofreader Michèle spots something missed many times. The second paragraph has the wrong (line) spacing – the space between the lines of text is narrower (a kind of textual 'stenosis'). Very few readers of this book would have noticed, and it's the kind of error even an experienced proofreader could overlook.

- On page 197, she also makes this observation. 'You leave a space for his [Archie's] picture, but he now appears on p. 199 with nothing on p. 198. Is this OK?' I describe this at the time as 'a wonderful query'. It's clever, too, being yet another simple item that's easily missed. The answer? There wasn't enough room for his picture on p. 197 (and if there were, I couldn't bear him to be separated from Eva); p. 198 cannot be used as Archie needs to be on 'art paper', which has to start on a new recto page, so he can only appear on the next page, 199!

- The proofreader comments (and this is a long entry so please skip if you like) in her latest query list re 'author–date system': 'I have used Harvard system in the Index with a cross-reference to author–date system, and you have a reference to both in the Glossary. I think it would be better to have under author–date system (*see Harvard system*) or something similar.' She is probably right, but I have now reached the latter stage complained of by her on p. 120. The author–date system is not *exactly* the same as the Harvard system, although apparently the two terms are used interchangeably. I have to own up and admit I mix them up sometimes. As far as I can remember, the author–date system refers to a referencing system, under which works are referred to by such designations as Denning (2006), cross-referenced to a bibliography. Some publishers prefer the 'short-title system'. Here, the first reference to a work may contain information on author, title of article, editor's name, book title, edition number, place of publication, date, volume number, page reference, and so forth, in that order. Second and subsequent references are shortened, and there are conventions that often apply, as to how to distinguish between a book by a single author, two books by a single author, one book edited by several authors, the citation of an article in a collection of essays by a single author, articles from journals, edition numbers. . . *Do not panic.* Style sheets often tell you all you need to know. The Harvard referencing system places a partial citation – the author's name and year of publication within parentheses – at the end of a sentence within the text (Denning 2006). There will be a complete citation at the end of the text in an alphabetical list of 'references'. If the author of the reference is named in the text itself, it's usual to put the date alone in parentheses, for example: 'Denning (2006) writes. . .' A page number may be shown like this (Denning 2006:187). Typically, references should include the author's name (not inverted, but depends on house style), title of the book or article, and the date of publication.

- The proofreader draws my attention on pp. 210 and 213 to (possible) inconsistent use of italic and roman for ibid., idem, and op. cit. I now have a wonderful excuse to leave them as they are, so that you, gentle reader, can find the inconsistencies, as I draw *your* attention to them.

- American usage: in the US, schedule is pronounced *skedule* but its *shedule* here. If you wanted to discuss this with a friend in the UK, you might use your mobile but in the US it would probably be on a cell phone.

- I've sometimes heard people say, 'I pacifically told him . . .' I tell them that it's nothing to do with the Pacific Ocean, and neither do they mean 'peacefully told him'; the word is 'specifically'.

- Incidentally, the proofreader makes a fine comment in her last list of queries regarding the use of *passim* ('in various places through-out the text'): 'It's a great shame that *passim* is gradually being weeded out of indexes. It used to be wonderful to use this for passing mentions of a subject, that didn't warrant subheadings, but avoided long strings of page numbers: 150–90 *passim*.'

- Michèle also tells me that there is a problem on p. 216 with *sic*. I have run into a few problems. She writes, 'This para. seems a bit inconsistent. You say (sic), then [sic], but I thought [sic] was for interpolation by author.' There's more but to answer this first. It sounds a bit like a line from an old song by George and Ira Gershwin: 'You like toh-mah-toh, I like toh-may-to'! We of course know that '*sic*' is a parenthetical comment on quoted words. It should be in italic (*New ODWE*), and means 'used or spelled as given'. The instance of '*sic*' on p. 216 in roman should therefore be changed to italic. This leaves only the question of round or square brackets.

- On the same page, the proofreader commented: 'The "*Sic* should not be used to sneer or scoff. . ." but that's precisely what is being done to Jade Goody. Can you clarify?' Last time I read about Jade Goody, she was splashed on the front page of a tabloid, claiming to be completely broke, even after a reputed £1m deal from a book publisher. It's a fact that some of her remarks have become legendary. 'Where's East Angular [*sic*] though? I thought that was somewhere abroad.' Am I using *sic* to scoff or sneer, or just reporting/repeating what other people have said? And were *they* scoffing or sneering? There isn't space enough to go through all the forms of usage but here are just two. Parentheses or round brackets ( ) are used for interpolations and remarks 'made by the writer of the text himself', e.g. 'I remain (as I always will be) true to my colours.' Square brackets [ ] are used for comments, corrections, explanations, or inter-polations, translations, etc., which were not in the original text, but added subsequently by others, be they authors or editors, or just plain 'others', e.g. 'Archie [that ugly old-fashioned bear] might have fallen for Eva in a big way, but the two were never introduced.' It is possible that the difference is still unclear; if that's so, please accept my apologies. (Now I know why. *I* wrote the sentence above, so the brackets should have been round. If someone else had written it, such an interpolation by me would have merited square brackets. If I awake tomorrow and decide to interpolate something (subsequently) into my own text, which should I use? I feel a page 120 feeling coming on.)

• Just as *The Pocket Book of Proofreading* is about to go to print, I have unexpectedly discovered two points in favour of Archie – in that 'old' reference books can sometimes be useful. While browsing through *ODWE* (1981), I am happy to see (when trying to fix a date for Darwin): **Darwin, Charles Robert,** 1809–82, author of *Origin of Species*. . . plus a separate entry for **Origin of Species (The),** by C. Darwin, 1859. In *New ODWE*, the separate entry for *The Origin of Species* has gone; **Darwin**[2] vies with **Darwin**[1] (the capital of Northern Territory, Australia). **Darwin**[1] Charles (Robert) (1809–82) is simply described as 'English natural historian'. There's no mention of his ship in *ODWE*, but in *New ODWE*, there is at least '*Beagle*' – 'ship on which Darwin travelled round the southern hemisphere'. Thus, the more modern *New ODWE* tells you nothing about evolution, about *The Origin of Species,* only that the English natural historian used a boat called the *Beagle* to swan around the southern hemisphere. Weird or what? *Shalott, The Lady of,* Tennyson's poem, not past its **shelf life** (two words), makes it into both but **date rape** (two words) is only found in *New ODWE*.

- My final reason for thinking that Archie perhaps should be saved from being stuck in one of those big glass cases, along with the 'old' reference books is that *ODWE* (1981) gave a lengthy four-page introduction on 'punctuation' – there was everything you could ever need on colons, semicolons, apostrophes, brackets, en rules and em rules, hyphens, parentheses, etc., and so forth. For example, it gave four uses for the em rule: no. 3 is 'to indicate pauses in hesitant speech, or the ending and resumption of a statement interrupted by the interlocutor. If the sentence is not interrupted but abandoned, use the ellipsis (q.v.)'. 'I think it's time to abandon this sentence now— no, changed my mind . . . ' *New ODWE* has no entry for 'punctuation' and says less about em and en rules. (I've now reinstated *ODWE* (1981), and it's *not* going into any big glass case.)
- This kind of work can sometimes be tiring, even trying, though ultimately it's usually rewarding. I'm happy to say that here's an antidote: the proofreader, Michèle Clarke, also the copy-editor and indexer for this book, has self-published one of her own, which is indeed a delight. It's her *A–Z of Kitchen and Garden Delights*, available for £4.00 plus 55p p&p. 'Lots of recipes and lots of information about garden plants, working through the alphabet' (contact mikindex@btinternet.com).

Don't I just know the talented Michèle is going to throw more things at me too, on the third and fourth reads! [The third set has just arrived back. I have been told off for being 'indeed too chatty', here and there, but on the whole it's not too bad. I'm happy. I begin to feel that I could agree with those lines in the film *Troy*, that *it's the gods who envy us* because we are alive on this sweet earth. . .] Perhaps it's time to let them go. Any further items must be left to pass like ships in the night. What really matters? That a sentence gently goes colon-less into that night? Or minus a comma where it matters? Who cares?

I think only of the poem by a forgotten poet, James Elroy Flecker (1884–1915), and his poem, 'To a Poet a Thousand Years Hence'. The poet writes that he cares not 'if you bridge the seas, or ride secure the cruel sky', or if you 'build consummate palaces of metal or of masonry'. More importantly, Flecker writes, 'But have you wine and music still, and statues and a bright-eyed love,' plus 'foolish thoughts of good and ill', and (pre-Dawkins – also Christopher Hitchens, author of *God Is Not Great*), 'prayers to them who sit above?' The poem ends beautifully:

> O friend unseen, unborn, unknown,
> Student of our sweet English tongue,
> Read out my words at night, alone:
> I was a poet, I was young.
>
> Since I can never see your face,
> And never shake you by the hand,
> I send my soul through time and space
> To greet you. You will understand.

The proofreader has lately sent me this note: 'Thanks – have collected all your notes and will start on these this week with a fair wind.'

To add your comments, please email:
editor@pocketbookofproofreading.co.uk

Index

PROOFREADING & COPY-EDITING COURSE

If you have enjoyed reading
The Pocket Book of Proofreading,
you can download the new and complete
Proofreading and Copy-editing Course
from www.learnfreelancing.com
or write for *free* details from the publisher:
The Managing Editor
PO Box 6885
Poole
BH4 0DH
Alternatively email your request to:
info@learnfreelancing.com

15610943R00146

Printed in Great Britain
by Amazon